Bonnet Girls

Patterns of the Past

Helen R. Scott

American Quilter's Society
P. O. Box 3290 • Paducah, KY 42002-3290
www.AQSquilt.com

Located in Paducah, Kentucky, the American Quilter's Society (AQS) is dedicated to promoting the accomplishments of today's quilters. Through its publications and events, AQS strives to honor today's quiltmakers and their work and to inspire future creativity and innovation in quiltmaking.

EDITOR: BARBARA SMITH
GRAPHIC DESIGN: LISA M. CLARK
COVER DESIGN: MICHAEL BUCKINGHAM
PHOTOGRAPHY: CHARLES R. LYNCH

Library of Congress Cataloging-in-Publication Data
Scott, Helen R.
      Bonnet girls : patterns of the past / by Helen R. Scott.
        p. cm.
      ISBN 1-57432-765-8
      1. Quilting--Patterns. 2. Appliqué--Patterns. 3. Embroidery--Patterns.
I. Title.
TT835 .S3592 2001
746.46'041--dc21   2001000489
                                               CIP

Additional copies of this book may be ordered from the American Quilter's Society, PO Box 3290, Paducah, KY 42002-3290, or online at www.AQSquilt.com.

Acknowledgments

I have been encouraged and helped by so many wonderful family members and friends, it is difficult to know where to start.

I am the only living child of Ruth and Glenn Bell who instilled in me the rewarding pleasures of drawing and quilting. My father helped me draw cartoons from newspapers and, together, Mother and I chose fabric for the dresses and quilts she made. Grandmother Simpson let me play under her quilting frame and was never too busy to explain her patterns and answer all my questions. Their quilts have warmed both me and my children.

Husband Jack understands my need to create and doesn't mind paints and paintings stacked in corners, and fabric and quilts overflowing tables, stuffed under beds, and tumbling from closets. Sons Jonathan and Thomas and daughter Rachel have requested quilts with birds, cats, flags, cars, butterflies, fish, and planets and have guided me in getting them exact and true to life.

Rev. Les Korselman urged me to teach my first quilting class in the church basement, and Linda Willis made space for classes in her fabric shop. My quilting, painting, and writing cohort, Mabel Massie, was always ready to listen and offer support. Ann Brandt's faith in my patterns and quilting methods and her willingness to invest her time in teaching them to others have made us friends.

All that I am is owed to my family and friends. They, in their own ways, have given me a part of themselves, and I am forever in their debt.

Contents

Introduction

Designing the patterns, selecting the fabrics, and sewing the quilt blocks for this book have given me much pleasure and satisfaction. If you played with and cherished dolls in your childhood, you will find that dressing the Bonnet Girls will bring back pleasant memories of that time.

My suggestions for colors and embellishments offered here are merely that. Your choices of fabric, color combinations, and embellishments will be entirely different from mine, and that is how it should be. Because the patterns do not require following the fabric grain, fat quarters and scraps are excellent sources of fabric.

The pages of props, such as fruit bowls, candlesticks, furniture, and animals, will help you create settings and themes for your blocks and quilts. Thumbnail sketches drawn by using the "X" method (page 23) will enable you to create special blocks. Use background quilting (page 110) or shadow appliqué (page 16) to add atmosphere and an original finish to your quilt.

The LITTLE QUILT and TULIP QUILT patterns (page 24) will give you the opportunity to do what quilters have always wanted to do...finish a quilt in one sitting.

Holiday themes in some patterns do not have to be followed. By changing the colors, props, and seasons, you can create your own setting. By quilting wind, rain drops, snowflakes, or clouds, you can control the weather.

The Bonnet Girls and their families are open to your ideas, situations, and plans for them. Have fun! Give your imagination free rein, and you will be pleasantly surprised with the results.

Part One

Getting Started

Choosing Fabrics

In choosing fabrics, I like to combine prints and solids, letting the colors in a print guide me to a solid companion fabric and embroidery floss. A plain white, cotton blend was the canvas on which I created my quilt blocks. You may want to use plain cotton, a cotton print, or even a pieced background fabric for your quilt.

Large plaids, checks, and stripes are not good choices for Bonnet Girl dresses. They do, however, lend themselves to trims on sleeves, collars, and bonnets. Large floral prints can be used as accents. Flowers can be needle-turn appliquéd to bonnets or dresses as embellishments.

Always consider using the wrong side of a fabric. Many times, it is better than the right side, or it can be used in conjunction with the right side. Small floral prints, checks, dots, geometric patterns, and shaded and solid-colored fabrics make beautiful clothing for Bonnet Girls. Fabrics should be washed to see if the dyes bleed.

The patterns were designed to celebrate busy, loving women. The fabric colors and embellishments used are only suggestions. You may want to exchange or add bonnets, props, or children to make a theme or family-tree quilt. The figures can be reversed or grouped as you desire.

Patterns

The Bonnet Girl patterns can be used at the size given or enlarged to create any size block. The quilts in the photos contain 14¼" x 21¼" blocks and 21¼" x 28½" blocks (finished sizes). Please read all notations in the patterns. Use a permanent pen to trace the pattern pieces onto transparent template plastic. Mark dashed lines, draping, embellishments, and other notations. Patterns for figures and props are drawn without turn-under allowances. Look at the whole pattern and make note of the places where pieces overlap. Mark x's along the covered edges to remind yourself to leave the allowances unturned. Write the pattern and figure name on each template. See-through plastic templates can be moved about on a floral or figured fabric to determine its appearance in the quilt block.

Store small pattern templates together in a small zippered bag with larger templates in a labeled, large plastic bag. Add embroidery floss, embellishments, and pattern notes. The in-progress block can be folded and tucked into this bag along with your sewing tools for a take-along project. Separate bags are useful for keeping two in-progress blocks apart.

Marking Fabric

Press fabrics before marking. On the right side of the fabric, draw around the template with a sharp pencil. A fine-line mechanical pencil always has a sharp point and can usually be erased with a kneaded rubber eraser. Mark dark fabrics with a white or silver pencil or a fine-line permanent marker. Indicate the edges that will not be turned under.

Cut out the fabric piece, adding a turn-under allowance by eye as you cut. Fold the allowance under on the marked line, leaving the appropriate edges unturned. Any pencil marks that are still visible after turning the allowance will be covered by embroidery stitches. To baste the allowance, use a thread in a contrasting color for easy removal. Place the basting thread knot on the right side of the fabric. Baste the entire piece, right side up; do not knot off. Press the pieces after they have been basted.

Positioning Figures

A poster-board template (referred to as a back guide) can be used as a guide for marking the sewing line on the backing fabric for each block (described under "Backing and batting" on page 17). The back guide is cut to the finished size of the block, so it provides an excellent "stage" for arranging your Bonnet Girls, other figures, and props. Pin or baste fabric pieces together as needed before placing them on the guide. You can move the fabrics easily over the smooth poster-board surface, and with this preview, you will be able to judge how your finished block will look.

You can also use the back guide to position your pieces on the background fabric. Cut the background the size needed plus 1½" all around for seam allowances because appliqué tends to draw up the block. Lay the back guide on a dark surface and center the background over the guide. The dark surface should be visible through the fabric on all four sides so you can see the block boundaries. Pin figures in place on the background fabric and baste securely.

If you are in doubt about positioning a bonnet or if you want to tilt a bonnet at a different angle, you can make a positioning guide, as follows: Make a plastic template from the head pattern (page 16). Place the template over the neck line of the dress and fit the bonnet over the head. Remove the template and stitch the bonnet in place.

Marking Details

Draping lines, creases, and folds add realism to your Bonnet Girls. These lines can be embroidered or drawn with fabric pens. Patterns for the Bonnet Girls were drawn first as human bodies before dresses, bonnets, and props were added. This drawing was important for determining fold and drape lines for figures in action. The easiest way to mark these clothing lines on your fabric is to use the side edge of the dress template as a guide. Remember that a skirt's folds and drapes come from the waist and fall downward. These lines can be marked after the figures have been pinned and basted together or after they have been basted on the background fabric. Just a few graceful lines

will add movement and dimension to the figures. In most cases, the curve of a bonnet edge can be used to mark the crown line.

Crease and tension lines for bodices and sleeves are also marked on each pattern. If you are in doubt about a shoulder or arm marking, use yourself as a model. Look in a mirror and note where the creases in your shirt fall, where they start and end, and the direction of the curves.

The Bonnet Girls are versatile. By using the props, you can easily change the block designs to suit your needs. Changing the positions of bonnets, arms, and hands will create movement and develop situations to fit your ideas. For instance, if you want to position an arm and hand reaching for a flower, you can simply change the lines of an existing pattern. There are many arm and hand patterns in this book, one of which may match the action you want to convey, with only minor adjustments.

If you can't find the right pattern, here is an easy way to draw one. Position your arm in front of a mirror. Look at the reflection and notice the angles. Start with a stick figure by drawing three straight lines: from shoulder to elbow, from elbow to wrist, and from wrist to fingertip. Then use shapes from one of the patterns to help flesh out the stick-figure arm.

If you can't find a hand pattern and want to draw one, place your hand between a bright light and a sheet of white paper. Position your hand as a unit with no protruding fingers or thumb, which would make appliqué difficult. Draw around the shadow of your hand. Reduce the drawing to the size needed. If the shape is correct, it isn't necessary to indicate fingers; however, with a little practice on paper, it can be done with just a few straight stitches. Again, use your own hand as a reference.

Background and Backing

Background and backing sizes are given in the patterns. The author's quilt-as-you-go Bonnet Girl blocks have 17" figures, which required large background and backing rectangles. Cutting with the lengthwise grain for either the single or the double blocks would have wasted fabric. Here's an easy way to cut these large background and backing pieces at the same time and save fabric.

Color Planning Chart
Make color notes or tape small fabric scraps to an enlarged copy of this chart to aid in selecting color and placing blocks.

single block

double block

Fig. 1–1. Cutting background and backing:

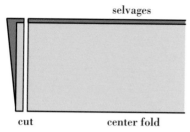

(a) Straighten one edge.

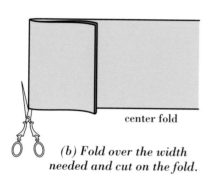

(b) Fold over the width needed and cut on the fold.

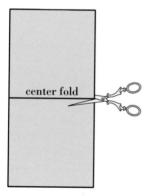

(c) Cut the background and backing pieces apart on the center fold.

1. Place a length of 45" fabric on a flat surface, folded with selvages together as it comes from the bolt.

2. Trim the leading edge perpendicular to the fold (Fig. 1–1a).

3. Fold the fabric back on itself the desired width of a single or a double block.

4. Gently press, then cut on fold (Fig. 1–1b).

5. Cut the background and backing pieces apart on the center fold (Fig. 1–1c). Single blocks are cut 15½" x 22½" and double blocks, 22½" x 29¾".

Embroidery Appliqué

Most appliqué patterns tell you to match the thread to the appliqué and sew the piece to the background with an invisible stitch. But for the Bonnet Girls, the appliqué stitches are part of the fun. You will want your appliqué to show, so choose contrasting embroidery floss and decorative embroidery stitches and enjoy!

1. Make a template by tracing the pattern onto transparent plastic. Cut on the traced line. Mark turn-under, overlap, and positioning lines on the template.

2. Draw around the template with a sharp pencil or marker on the right side of the fabric.

3. Cut out the fabric piece, adding a ³⁄₁₆"–¼" turn-under allowance by eye all around.

4. Turn under the allowance on the pencil line and baste it in place. Press.

5. Using the pattern pages and templates as guides, pin or baste the appliqué pieces for each figure or prop together.

6. Position and baste pieces to the pressed background rectangle. Use the edges of the templates to mark the fold and guide lines on the figures.

7. Use embroidery stitches to appliqué the figures to the background. Sew through all fabric thicknesses, as close as possible to the turn-under fold.

Embroidery floss – Artists paint motion, depth, and atmosphere on a flat canvas with line, color, and brush strokes. The embroidery needle and floss can do the same with stitches and color on a flat quilt block.

Have on hand a large palette of floss in a range of colors and values from light to dark. Select a variety of bright, muted, and dark colors that you consider beautiful and even some you think are ugly. That terrible color may be just the one needed to set off a print fabric that can't be classified into any color category.

Choosing the right color. After the appliqué pieces have been basted to the background fabrics, lay several lengths of darker or contrasting floss along the edges to be embroidered. Choose the floss color that complements both the appliqué and the background fabric.

Keep in mind that black floss can appear harsh and cold. In most cases, navy blue or dark brown is a better choice. Ecru is bright and warm and can be used if white seems too dull.

If the fabric is dark, choose a floss of an entirely different color, such as a medium shade of red or green on dark blue fabric, rust or orange on dark brown, and blue or green on red. Bright gold or green-gold tones can be used on most dark fabrics. Variegated brown, rust, and yellow floss are excellent choices for making floss hair.

Rayon floss. Many beautiful, shining colors and shades can be found in rayon floss. It is a little difficult to use, but it produces results that make it well worth the effort. Running the floss through beeswax makes stitching easier. One or two strands can be used for most embroidery. If a heavier line of stitching is desired, use the running stitch or scalloped woven stitches, described on page 12. Double one or two strands of floss in your needle and knot the ends together.

Metallic floss. Metallics are wonderful for rings, bracelets, and earrings, and for trimming dresses and bonnets. Silver floss adds sparkle to Fourth of July sparklers and produces a bright highlight when braided or twisted with dark floss to complement a hair style. Use metallics for woven embroidery stitches, floss hair styles, and cords. Thread the needle with short lengths and watch for knotting and wear.

Embroidery tips

• *Make stitches as close to the turned-under edges of the appliqué as possible.*

• *Use a thin, sharp needle, such as an embroidery, embroidery/crewel, or quilting needle.*

• *Pull floss, one strand at a time, from cut 16" to 18" lengths.*

• *A small embroidery hoop will help control the stitches and keep the work flat.*

• *Use small knots to begin and end the floss on the wrong side of the quilt block. Clip off excess floss.*

• *Practice making even stitches and be careful not to pull them too tight.*

• *Use beeswax if floss twists or is hard to pull through the fabric.*

• *Use smaller stitches on sharp points and tight curves.*

• *Floss can become fuzzy and break. Knot off if it appears worn.*

• *Press blocks, embroidery side down, on a soft towel placed on an ironing board.*

• *Learn a variety of stitches and use them to embellish your appliqué.*

Fig. 1–2. Simple embroidery stitches:

(a) Running stitch.

(b) Even-line woven stitch.

(c) Scalloped woven stitch.

(d) Stem or outline stitch.

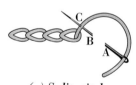

(e) Split stitch.

(f) Straight stitches.

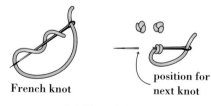

French knot   position for
                     next knot

(g) French knots.

Floss variations. Combine two or three shades of one color in your needle. A strand of lighter floss will add highlights to your stitches. Combine two or three different colors for a variegated or tweedy look. Try using two shades or colors for sewing French knots for buttons and other embellishments.

Embroidery stitches – A small embroidery hoop, 4", 5", or 6", provides better control over needle and floss. Use thin, sharp needles with long eyes. Two or three strands of floss can be used for most embroidery. Note the number of strands used in the illustrations.

Using embroidery appliqué for the patterns in this series offers many opportunities for trying a variety of embroidery stitches. Beginners will find that the following simple stitches will produce beautiful blocks.

Running stitch. Use two or three strands of floss that are darker than the appliqué or that contrast with it. Place small, even running stitches as close as possible along the turned-under edge of the appliqué pieces (Fig. 1–2a). Sew through all thicknesses.

For the woven stitch, start with a running stitch. With the same or contrasting floss, weave under the floss only, not the fabric. An even-line woven stitch (Fig. 1–2b) can be used for an entire block or combined with a scalloped woven stitch (Fig. 1–2c) to embellish a cuff, collar, bonnet, or skirt edge.

Stem or outline stitch. This stitch makes a smooth outline (Fig. 1–2d). It can be varied by the number and colors of strands used in the needle. It can also be woven for a more textured look. A split stitch can also be used for outlines (Fig. 1–2e).

Straight stitches. Vary the length and direction of the stitches to create fringe, hair, leaves, and twigs (Fig. 1–2f).

French knots. Use these knots for buttons, beads, or snowflakes (Fig. 1–2g).

Embellishments

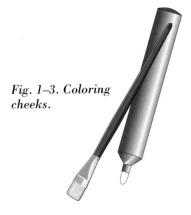

Fig. 1–3. Coloring cheeks.

Pink cheeks — To give the women and children a natural look, the following method was devised by teacher and quilter Ann M. Brandt. Tint the cheeks after the features are marked on the fabric but before the piece is cut out and before it is appliquéd and embroidered.

You will need a red, fine-point permanent marker and a ¼" or ½" artist's bristle brush. Pass the brush lightly, three or four times, over the marker point. Test the brush on paper or a scrap of flesh-toned fabric to determine the amount of color on the brush. Brush the cheek area with light strokes to gradually build up color (Fig. 1–3).

Fig. 1–4. Straight hair.

Floss hair — Floss strands, made into braids, twists or curls, can be used to replace any of the bun hair patterns.

Straight. Cut eight 4¼" lengths of floss. Tie them together in the center with thread. Sew the tied end under the edge of the appliquéd portion of the hair or bonnet. Trim the bottom ends of the hair even (Fig. 1–4).

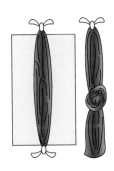

Fig. 1–5. Pony tail.

Pony tail. Cut eight 6" lengths of floss. Tie them together in the center with thread. Place the tied ends under the appliquéd hair or a bonnet. Add a ribbon, lace, floss tie, or bow. Trim the bottom ends (Fig. 1–5).

Fig. 1–6. Knotted hair.

Knotted. Wrap a 4" piece of poster board five times with floss. Tie the loops at the top and bottom edges of the poster board with thread. Remove the floss from the board and tie it in a knot. Trim the bottom edges even (Fig. 1–6).

Twisted. Wrap three yards of floss around a 3" piece of poster board. Tie the loops with thread at the top and bottom edges of the poster board. Remove the floss from the board. Twist the floss three or four times and tie the two looped ends together (Fig. 1–7). Place the tied ends under the edge of appliquéd hair or a bonnet and tack in place with one strand of matching floss.

Fig. 1–7. Twisted hair.

3" Braided. Cut ten 10" lengths of floss. Fold the lengths in half and tie the center with thread. Pin the loop ends to something stationary. Divide the floss into three sections and braid. Tie the cut end with ribbon or floss. Trim the cut ends (Fig. 1–8).

Fig. 1–8. Braided hair.

Fig. 1–9. Curled hair:

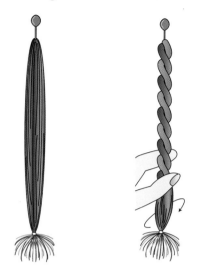

(a) Fold floss lengths in the center.   (b) Twist the floss.

(c) Pinch twisted floss ½" from secured end.   (d) Let floss twist back on itself to form the curl.

Fig. 1–10. Fold and tie floss.

Curls

• Cut two 24" lengths of floss. (Increase the number of floss lengths for heavier hair styles.) Fold the lengths in the center and knot the cut ends together (Fig. 1–9a).

• Pin the loop ends to something stationary. Twist the floss tightly, in one direction, until the floss doubles back on itself when the tension is relaxed (Fig. 1–9b).

• Hold the floss taut with the right hand. With the left hand, pinch the twisted floss ½" from the secured end (Fig. 1–9c).

• Let it twist back on itself to form a "curl" (Fig. 1–9d). Repeat pinching and twisting until the entire length is curled.

• Place the knot and tied loop ends under a bonnet or the appliquéd hair and stitch in place.

• Arrange the curls and tack them to the fabric with one strand of matching floss.

Tassels — Embroidery floss can be used to make tassels, cords, and belts or decorations for bonnets and handbags.

Cut three or four 4" lengths of floss. (Use more and longer strands of floss for larger tassels.) Fold the floss in half. With cut ends together, tie a knot and slide it close to the looped end (Fig. 1–10). Trim the cut ends even. Catching all the looped ends, sew the tassel to the appliqué.

Cords — The length of a finished cord depends on how tightly it is twisted and the number of floss lengths used. Floss lengths cut approximately six times longer than the finished cord will come close to the desired finished length.

To make multicolored cords, combine different shades and colors. You can also use variegated or metallic floss in your cords. Use longer lengths of floss for longer cords. Add more lengths of floss for heavier cords.

• Cut one length of six-strand floss 12" long. Fold the length in half and pin the loop ends to something stationary.

• Hold the cut ends, keeping the floss taut, and twist until the floss starts to double back on itself when tension is relaxed (Fig. 1–11a).

• With the left hand, pinch twisted floss in the center (Fig. 1–11b).

• Guide the twisting floss back to the pin (Fig. 1–11c).

• Remove the floss from the pin. Hold the ends tightly and use a single thread to tie the cut end. Repeat for the looped end.

• If you would like a tassel on the end of the cord, tie a knot in the cord at the cut end and slide the knot to the desired position before tightening it. Trim the cut ends even (Fig. 1–12).

Lace and ribbons —

If you are undecided about colors, ribbons, and laces for your Bonnet Girls, television can help. Period movies, such as Westerns, pioneer movies, and Civil War films, can give you ideas. Keep a small sketch pad and pencil with your sewing supplies and make quick sketches and color notes on clothing, embellishments, and backgrounds.

Lace. As with embroidery floss, having a large selection of laces and ribbons to choose from will add to your ability to enhance appliquéd figures. Laces from ¼" to 6" in width, gathered, straight, and beaded, can be used on bonnets, skirts, and aprons.

If gathered lace is used under the edge of an appliquéd piece, it is best to remove the heading and regather the lace with a single thread to eliminate bulk. If lace is used on top of an appliquéd piece, gather the lace with matching thread and attach it with decorative embroidery stitches and contrasting floss.

Wide lace can be trimmed along the straight edge and secured under the edge of an appliquéd piece.

For a rosette, use a running stitch along the straight edge of any width of lace. Pull the thread to gather the lace and tack the raw edges together.

Seam binding. Commercial binding can be used to make delicate bows for bonnets and aprons. Streamers on aprons or bonnets can be tacked in graceful curves to appear wind-blown or they can be left hanging free. The streamers can also be outline quilted for a dimensional look.

Ribbon. Ribbon can be used alone or in conjunction with lace. Run small gathering stitches, with matching thread or floss, down the center along the length of the ribbon (Fig. 1–13). Gather and tack the ribbon in place on a dress or bonnet or use the gathered ribbon in hair. You can also make a rosette, as with lace (Fig. 1–14).

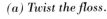

Fig. 1–11. Cords:

(a) Twist the floss.   *(b) Pinch the twisted floss in the center.*

(c) Guide the twisting floss back to the pin.

Fig. 1–12. Cord with tassel.

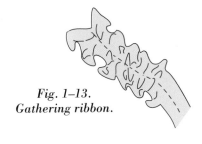

Fig. 1–13. Gathering ribbon.

Fig. 1–14. Forming a ribbon rosette.

Bonnet embellishing ideas.

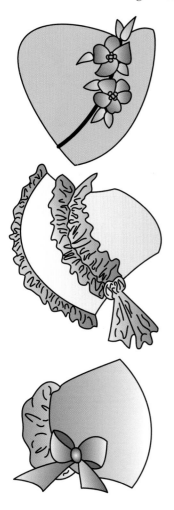

Twist two different colors of ribbon together and tack the twist to a dress, bonnet, or hair. Braid three colors together. Tie ribbon in knots, clusters of two or three knots together, or in bows. Use these with long streamers on aprons or bonnets. Bows can also be used for braids and pony tails.

In most cases, bows, streamers, and knotted ribbon can be tacked in place after the block has been quilted. This will keep them from becoming wrinkled during the constant handling required for quilting. Treat cut edges with a sealant to prevent fraying.

Shadow appliqué –

Shadow appliqué has been used in the background behind several figures. To see if a fabric can be used for shadow appliqué, place a white fabric on a flat surface. Lay colored, striped, and floral pieces on the fabric. Cover them with a piece of the background fabric to test the degree of shadowing through the background. If your background fabric is not sheer enough for this method, consider using embroidery, piecing, fabric paint, or printed fabric to create mood instead.

Clear colors are best for shadow appliqué: yellow, orange, pink, turquoise, light blue, and green. Darker colors will appear gray. Dark blue, gray, or purple can be used to indicate a cloudy day. Striped or floral shadow appliqué can be used for indoor settings. Quilt on the stripes and around the flowers.

To determine where you want to place the shadow appliqué, make thumbnail sketches before lightly drawing the lines on the shadow fabric (Fig.1–15).

The following shadow appliqué example describes how to create the appearance of a blue sky and clouds on a sunny day. Use clear light blue or turquoise as the shadow fabric (Fig. 1–16).

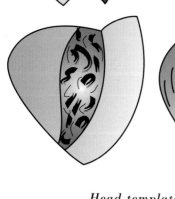
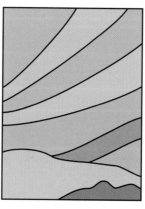

Head template, as described on page 8.

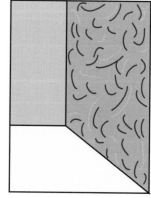

Fig. 1–15. Thumbnail sketches for shadow appliqué.

• Complete all the embroidery appliqué first. Press the block, right side down, on a soft towel.

• Cut out cloud shapes from the blue sky fabric. Discard the cloud shapes.

• Position the remaining blue sky pieces on the block and baste. (Do not turn under the edges of the blue pieces.)

• Trim the blue sky fabric from behind the appliquéd figures, ¼" inside the embroidered edges.

• Prepare the block for quilting as described on page 18.

• Quilt the block as desired, stitching through the blue shadow fabric to hold it in place.

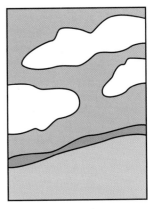

Fig. 1–16. Shadow appliqué example.

Quilt as You Go

With this method, each block is layered and quilted, and the edges are finished before the blocks are sewn together. You can assemble them one or two at a time as you finish them, or you can wait and join them all at once.

Backing and batting

• For each quilt block, cut one 15½" x 22½" piece of batting and two 15½" x 22½" pieces of fabric for the top and the backing.

• To make a back guide for marking the backing fabric, cut a piece of poster board 14¼" x 21¼". For a double block, cut two single poster-board pieces, place them long sides together, and secure with tape. The double-block guide can be folded to serve for a single block.

• Center the back guide on the wrong side of the backing fabric, leaving a seam allowance showing on all sides.

• Draw around the back guide with a sharp pencil (Fig. 1–17). The pencil line is the stitching line.

Block assembly

• Place the batting on a flat surface. Cover it with the pressed block, appliquéd side up.

• Cover the appliquéd block with the pressed backing fabric, marked side up (Fig. 1–18). Check to see that the pencil lines

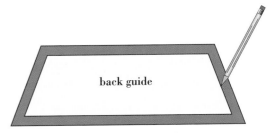

back guide

Fig. 1–17. Use the guide to mark the stitching line on the wrong side of the backing.

Fig. 1–18. Layered block.

Fig. 1–19. Pin the block every 1½" to 2".

cover the appliqué and the edges of the fabric underneath. Pin the edges through all thicknesses at 3" to 4" intervals.

• With a sewing machine, start at the center of the 21½" side, backstitch three or four stitches, and sew on the pencil line around the entire block. Stop 6" to 7" from the starting point and backstitch three or four stitches.

• Trim the allowances to ¼" and cut the corner seam allowances diagonally just outside the seam line about ¹⁄₁₆".

• Insert your hand in the opening and turn block right side out.

• Push out seams and corners, then baste ¼" in from all the edges.

• Turn in edges of opening, even with the block edges, and baste.

• Smooth out the block and pin at 3" to 4" intervals (Fig. 1–19).

• Baste securely in a 1½"–2" grid. Remove pins.

• Whip stitch the opening closed or leave it open if that edge will be joined to another block. Whip stitching the two blocks together will close the opening.

Quilting

Because the blocks are set side by side without sashing, the various quilting designs will clash where the blocks are joined. To solve this problem, a "frame" can be quilted around each block.

Quilted frame

After the block has been basted, use a ruler and pencil to draw a line ⅜" from the outside edges of the block. This quilted line will cover and hold the turned-in seam allowance. Mark another quilting line 1" in from the ⅜" line. Mark diagonal lines from the inside corners of the ⅜" line to the 1" corners to create the appearance of miters (Fig. 1–20).

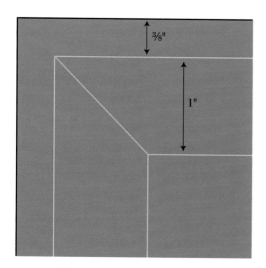

Fig. 1–20. Mark frame quilting lines.

Background – Just as sky, hills, mountains, trees, and water create mood in a painting, so can quilting convey mood in a quilt. Background quilting ideas are included with some of the block patterns to help you create atmosphere. For example, the wind template on page 110 can be turned end for end and reversed. Use it to draw slanted irregularly spaced lines to indicate a windy day or set it vertically to convey a calm, peaceful atmosphere. Other background quilting suggestions are given in the Bonnet Girls patterns, and the quilting patterns on page 110 will provide you with a variety of designs to choose from.

Trace quilting patterns onto transparent plastic and cut them out to use as templates. Mark guide lines and notations on the templates. Planning your design is much easier if you start on a plain sheet of paper cut the dimensions of the area to be quilted. Working from the center outward or from the left and right edges toward the center for a balanced design, trace the templates on the paper. Use a fine-line mechanical pencil and mark slowly to avoid over marking at points. Use a transparent ruler if you want to draw parallel or grid lines on the background.

Sculpture quilting – The turned, basted, and marked block is ready to be quilted, and because of the close basting, it is not necessary to use a quilting hoop. Start quilting near the center of the block, rolling the edge up and over the appliquéd top like a scroll. Rolling the block this way will keep the backing flat and free of puckers.

To create a sculptured look, quilt as close as possible around each appliquéd piece. The figures and props will then stand out against the quilted background. Quilting along drape lines gives a padded appearance. Tiny top-quilting stitches sewn close to and nearly under embroidered drape lines create dimension but are virtually invisible.

Remove all basting stitches except those ¼" from the outside edges of the block. They hold the edges together. You can remove them after the blocks have been whip stitched together.

Joining Blocks

- Arrange the quilted blocks on a flat surface.

- Pin the first two blocks together at the corners through all thicknesses.

- Pull the edges to straighten them and then pin them together along the edge to be sewn. The top and backing edges of both blocks should be visible and even (Fig. 1–21).

- Whip stitch the edges together with matching quilting thread. (See Whip Stitching on page 20.)

Fig. 1–21. Joining blocks.

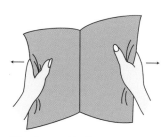

Fig. 1–22. Pull joined blocks sharply to set the stitches.

• Pull the joined blocks sharply to make the stitches fall between the blocks (Fig. 1–22). No stitches or spaces should be visible on the quilt top. If stitches show, they have not been pulled tightly enough. If spaces show, the stitches should be closer together.

• Assemble the blocks in horizontal rows. If the sewn strips appear soiled from handling, you can wash them at this time. Then sew the rows together.

Finishing – A quilt or wallhanging made by the quilt-as-you-go method has no raw edges and could be considered finished after assembly. If you like, you can weave the ⅜" quilted frame line with embroidery floss or narrow binding, or you can add a traditional binding.

Whip Stitching

Catch only two or three threads from each of the four block edges. Do not overlap stitches. You will need about 25 stitches to the inch. Use short lengths of thread and watch for wear. If the thread becomes frayed, knot off in the batting as you would for hand quilting. The whipped edges should feel flat, with no ridge, when opened.

Although the following stitching method may be a little awkward at first, with a little practice, it will become natural and comfortable.

Work from right to left. Hold your left hand with the palm up. Place the pinned edge of the block between your index and middle fingers. Turn your hand to the position shown in Fig. 1–23 and pinch the block edges between your index finger and thumb. Whip stitch from the upper-right corner, removing pins as you sew. Join corners with "X" stitches (Fig. 1–24).

Fig. 1–23. Pinch the block edges with the left hand and whip stitch from right to left.

Fig. 1–24. Join four corners with an "X."

Prop Patterns

Do you remember playing with paper dolls? I do. My friends and I would sit on the front porch for hours cutting, fitting, and talking for these little flat friends. We found old catalogs and cut out dresses that came close to the shape of our dolls. We made dresses from paper and colored them. Our imaginations soared and our hearts were content. Now that I've grown too old for paper dolls, I find that remembered pleasure in dressing Bonnet Girls. I sincerely hope that you will too.

Using Props

The props presented on pages 24–27 are a collection of familiar objects designed to be held or used by Bonnet Girls to change the setting or theme of a quilt or quilt block. Look through the patterns with the knowledge that the figures can be reversed. The figures and props can can also be traded, combined, or omitted. Change the positions of arms and hands to hold a tea cup, candle, or purse. Combine two figures for a tea party or quilting bee.

With very few changes, you can alter the actions and settings of your Bonnet Girls (Fig. 2–1). For instance, Rachel, without the baby, can carry a birthday cake. Karen can take a break from her sewing for a cup of tea, and Isabella can show you her new lace handkerchief.

Rachel

Karen

Isabella

Fig. 2–1. Pattern variations.

Miss Janet

April Rose

Allegra

Fig. 2–1. Pattern variations, cont.

Fig. 2–2. Combined patterns.

Finished Little Quilts.

Combining Patterns and Props

I'm sure you will think of many ways to combine patterns and props. The sketch in Fig. 2–2 makes use of several patterns: the clothes line from Leah's block; items from the prop pages to hang on the line; and Norma, Luke, and dog, Massie, from other patterns. To plan your block, see The "X" Drawing Method on page 23.

Little Quilt – The Little Quilt pattern on page 24 can be used in a number of ways. It can be held in the hand of one girl, shared and held by two, laid across the lap of a seated figure, hung on a clothes line, draped on a carriage, or placed on the arm of a rocking chair.

Planning is important. Decide on the positioning of the figures or props to accommodate the quilt's size. Determine if the figures' arms should be raised or lowered to hold the quilt. The little quilt can be held either horizontally or vertically between two Bonnet Girls. Only the upper edge is tacked to the block.

Little Quilt Pattern (page 24)
7¾" x 6¼"

• Trace the body of the quilt and each border to make templates. Cut the templates on the traced lines.

• Trace the templates on the right side of the fabric. Place the border pieces on the bias to accommodate the curves.

• Cut out the pieces, adding ¼" seam allowances, except you will want to add ½" to the outer edges of the borders for finishing the quilt. Sew the borders to the quilt.

• Appliqué or embroider the center of the quilt if desired.

• Cut the quilt backing and half a thickness of batting the size of the finished quilt.

• Baste the layers together and quilt as desired.

• Turn the border edges to the back, turn under an allowance, and blind stitch.

Use the following method to construct a block with the Little Quilt:

• Baste the fabric figures together and position them on the quilt block with the finished and quilted Little Quilt under their hands. Set the Little Quilt aside.

• Complete appliqué and quilt the block, leaving hands unsewn. Place the Little Quilt corners under the hands and stitch the hands in place. Tack only the top edge of Little Quilt to the block.

Tulip Quilt —
The tulips on this three-dimensional quilt can be embroidered or appliquéd. Appliqué the top of the quilt under the hand of one of the Bonnet Girls. The quilt hangs free of the block.

Tulip Quilt Pattern (page 24)
3½" x 4¾"

• Use floral, hand-pieced, or solid fabric for the quilt top, cut 7" x 9". Cut the backing 7" x 9" also.

• Trace the pattern outline on backing fabric (Fig. 2–3). If print fabric is used for the backing, trace the pattern on the wrong side.

• Place half a thickness of batting on a flat surface. Cover the batting with the quilt top fabric, right side up, and the backing, marked side up. Baste around the quilt just inside the traced line.

• Sew through all thicknesses from A to B (Fig. 2–4). Trim close to seam. Turn right side out and whip stitch the opening closed.

• Quilt as desired. The quilt can be embellished with embroidery or lace.

Finished Tulip Quilts.

Fig. 2–3. Trace the pattern on the backing piece.

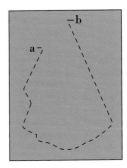

Fig. 2–4. Sew on the line, leaving an opening between A and B.

The "X" Drawing Method
Start planning your block by making small sketches to work out your idea. Even if you can't draw, you can use the "X" method. Simply draw a large X with the top shorter than the bottom. Close the top and bottom with slightly curved lines and add an oval head and stick arms. Draw a rectangle around the figure or figures to represent the block.

(a) Draw a large X.

(b) Close the top and bottom.

(c) Add a rectangle.

Cut templates on the line. Add ³⁄₁₆"–¼" allowances, by eye, to fabric pieces.

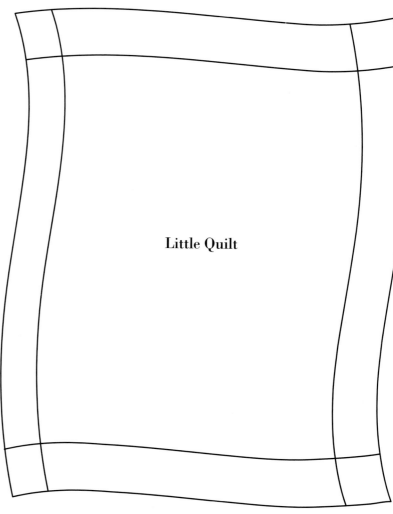

Little Quilt

Tulip Quilt

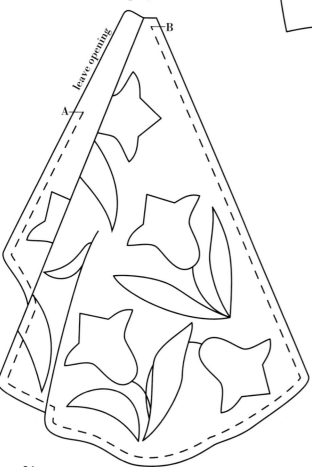

leave opening

A—

B

Allegra

Small quilt patterns: Instructions for these props begin on page 22.

Satin stitch clothespins.

Embroider flowers and other details.

Bonnet Girls — Patterns of the Past   Helen R. Scott

Purse

Gather top and embroider
handle over arm or in hand

*Use embroidery
stitches (page 12)
for details, such as
wrought iron, facial
features, flowers,
and wood grain.*

Part Three

Block

Patterns

Ruby

While working on a Bonnet Girl design, I try to picture the finished block. This pattern, to me, called for red, and as I worked on the embroidery, Ruby seemed just right for her name.

Red rayon floss was used to accent her bonnet, cuff edges, bustle, and the bottom of her skirt with a row of split stitches. One strand of rayon floss was woven into the edge of the lace that trims her parasol. Embroidery floss curls pick up the soft tones of her parasol. Fabric could be used for her hair instead.

The ⅜" ribbon trim on Ruby's bonnet was gathered with a running stitch through the center. Knot the ribbon at the top, turn under the raw edge at bottom and tack in place with matching floss or thread. Gold metallic floss accents her lace collar, ring, and parasol handle. The birds are shadow appliquéd.

Fabric Requirements

Small patterns (as given): Use scraps for appliqué and embellishments. Block finishes 9½" x 14". Cut background, backing, batting 11" x 15½".

Enlarged patterns (155%): Use fabric measurements below. Block finishes 14¼" x 21¼". Cut background, backing, batting 15½" x 22½".

Figure / Fabric

Ruby

Figure	Fabric
Skirt, sleeves, and bonnet	12" x 12"
Overskirt, bustle, bonnet facing	12" x 10"
Gloves	2" x 5"
Hair	2" x 2"

Props

Parasol	7" x 7"

Shadow appliqué

Birds	3" x 4"

Embroidery

Bonnet, cuff edges, bustle, and skirt
Collar, ring, and parasol handle
Parasol
French knot buttons for bodice

Embellishments

16" of ½" lace for dress
12" of ⅜" ribbon for bonnet
18" of 1" lace for parasol
2" of ½" lace for collar

Gathered and
knotted ribbon

Bonnet and hair

Lace

Bodice

Techniques
Embroidery Appliqué, p. 10
Embroidery Tips, p. 11
Embroidery Stitches, p. 12
Hair, p. 13
Tassels and Cords, p. 14
Lace and Ribbons, p. 15
Shadow Appliqué, p. 16

Overskirt

Lace

Skirt

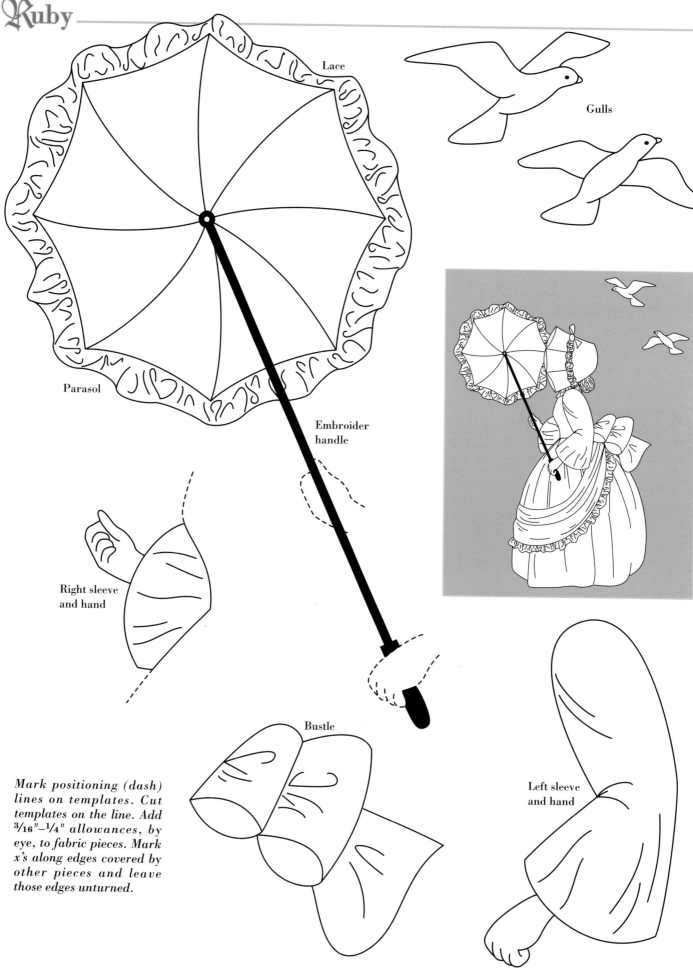

Lace

Gulls

Parasol

Embroider
handle

Right sleeve
and hand

Left sleeve
and hand

Bustle

Mark positioning (dash) lines on templates. Cut templates on the line. Add ³/₁₆"–¹/₄" allowances, by eye, to fabric pieces. Mark x's along edges covered by other pieces and leave those edges unturned.

Helen R. Scott   Bonnet Girls – Patterns of the Past

A Summer's Day
*Morning broke
with crimson-red glory,
beckoning those inspired
to seek pen and brush
in feeble attempts
to copy God.*

Augusta can't resist dipping her toes into the inviting blue ocean. Being a demure old-fashioned girl, she wears pantaloons. I chose lace to match the lace on her bonnet. You may want to use fabric like her bodice or skirt or be daring and leave her legs bare.

Tranquil soft clouds were quilted on the white background fabric with shadow appliqué blue sky. Quilting lines around the shadow-appliquéd gulls were woven with one strand of blue-gray floss. You can embroider or appliqué the gulls, if you prefer. The sky is quilted to represent softly rounded clouds. The inquisitive fish was satin stitched with rayon floss to give him a shiny, wet look.

Fabric Requirements

Small patterns (as given): Use scraps for appliqué and embellishments. Block finishes 9½" x 14". Cut background, backing, batting 11" x 15½".

Enlarged patterns (155%): Use fabric measurements below. Block finishes 14¼" x 21¼". Cut background, backing, batting 15½" x 22½".

Figure	Fabric
Augusta	
Skirt and sleeve	10" x 12"
Bodice	4" x 5"
Neck, arm, and legs	7" x 11"
Hair	3" x 3"
Bonnet	5" x 5"
Props	
Ocean	6" x 11"
Gulls	4" x 6"
Other	
Shadow fabric	8" x 12"

Embroidery
Fish
Gulls

Embellishments
6" of 6" lace or fabric for pantaloons
5" of 1¼" gathered lace for bonnet
8" of ⅜" ribbon for bonnet

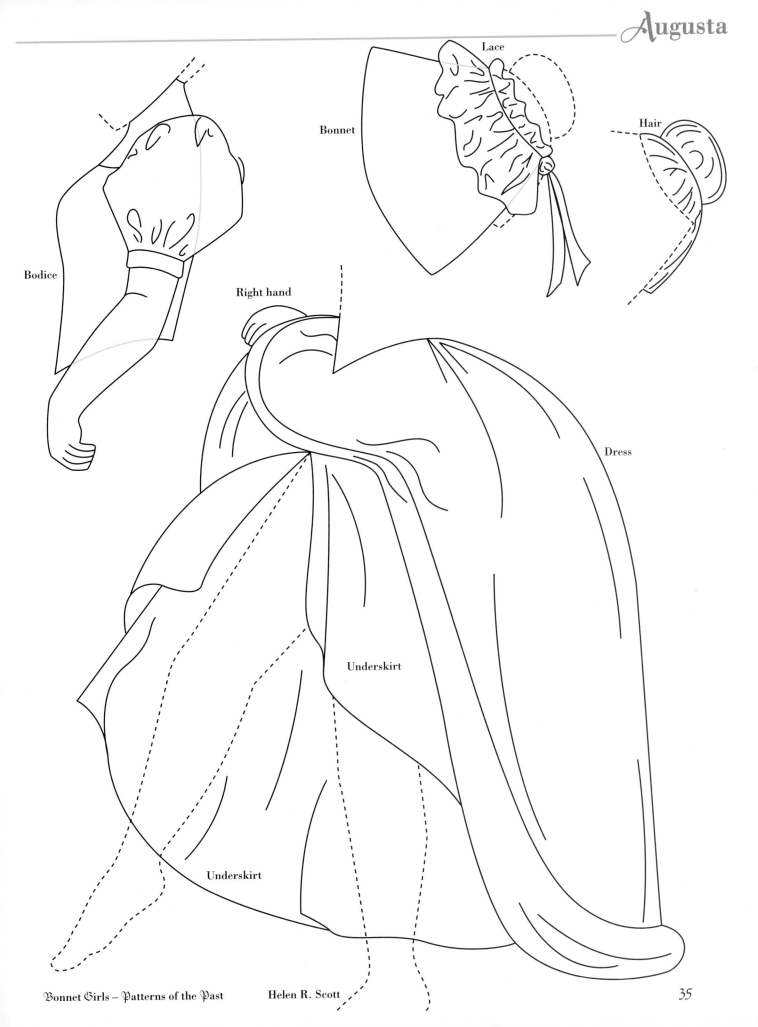

Bodice

Bonnet

Lace

Hair

Right hand

Dress

Underskirt

Underskirt

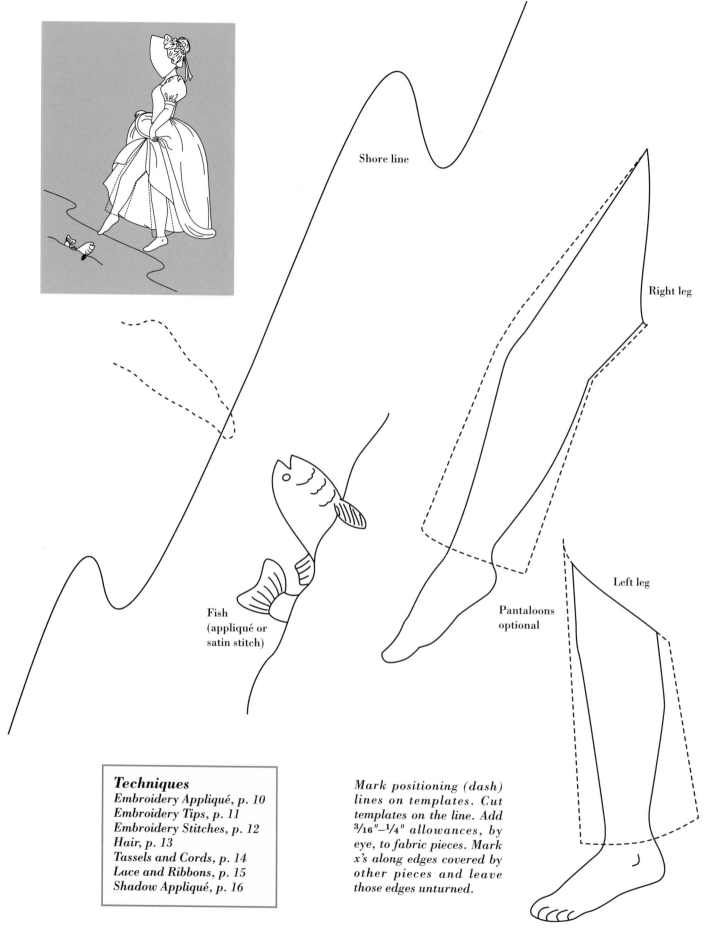

Shore line

Right leg

Fish
(appliqué or
satin stitch)

Pantaloons
optional

Left leg

Techniques
Embroidery Appliqué, p. 10
Embroidery Tips, p. 11
Embroidery Stitches, p. 12
Hair, p. 13
Tassels and Cords, p. 14
Lace and Ribbons, p. 15
Shadow Appliqué, p. 16

*Mark positioning (dash)
lines on templates. Cut
templates on the line. Add
³/₁₆"–¹/₄" allowances, by
eye, to fabric pieces. Mark
x's along edges covered by
other pieces and leave
those edges unturned.*

Allegra

As with its companion block, Hannah (page 50), the three figures are set against a background of shadow-appliquéd sky, hills, and river. To enhance the colors, quilted lines around these areas were whip stitched with one strand of matching embroidery floss.

The hill reflection on the river was achieved with acrylic paint. Use a thin blue-green mixture of paint and water and a small bristle brush. Dip the dry brush lightly in the paint mixture, test on scrap fabric, and brush short vertical strokes 1" to 1½" long. Random horizontal strokes in mid-river were embroidered with white floss to represent waves. The river was painted after quilting. You may prefer to paint at an earlier stage.

Allegra could be used alone on a smaller block. Give her a quilt to work on and set her under a tree borrowed from Hannah, or join the two river blocks for a panel wallhanging.

Fabric Requirements

Small patterns (as given): Use scraps for appliqué and embellishments. Block finishes 14" x 19". Cut background, backing, batting 15½" x 20½".

Enlarged patterns (155%): Use fabric measurements below. Block finishes 21¼" x 28½". Cut background, backing, batting 22½" x 30".

Figure	Fabric
Faces and hands	5" x 5"
Allegra	
Blouse	5" x 5"
Skirt	6" x 12"
Bonnet	5" x 5"
Book	3" x 2"
Slipper	1" x 1"
Albert	
Shirt	6" x 7"
Vest	6" x 7"
Pants	6" x 9"
Shoes	4" x 4"
Hair	4" x 4"

Aaron	
Shirt	6" x 6"
Pants	3" x 6"
Hair	3" x 3"
Shoes	2" x 3"
Hat	2" x 3"
Grassy rocks	scraps
Props	
Tree foliage	9" x 11"
Branches	2" x 4"
Shadow fabric	
Hills	6" x 14"
Water	5" x 19"
Sky	12" x 18"
Embroidery	
Eagle	
Water	

Embellishments

6" of ¾" lace for neck, and cuff

3" of ¼" ribbon for bonnet

3" or ⅛" ribbon for hair

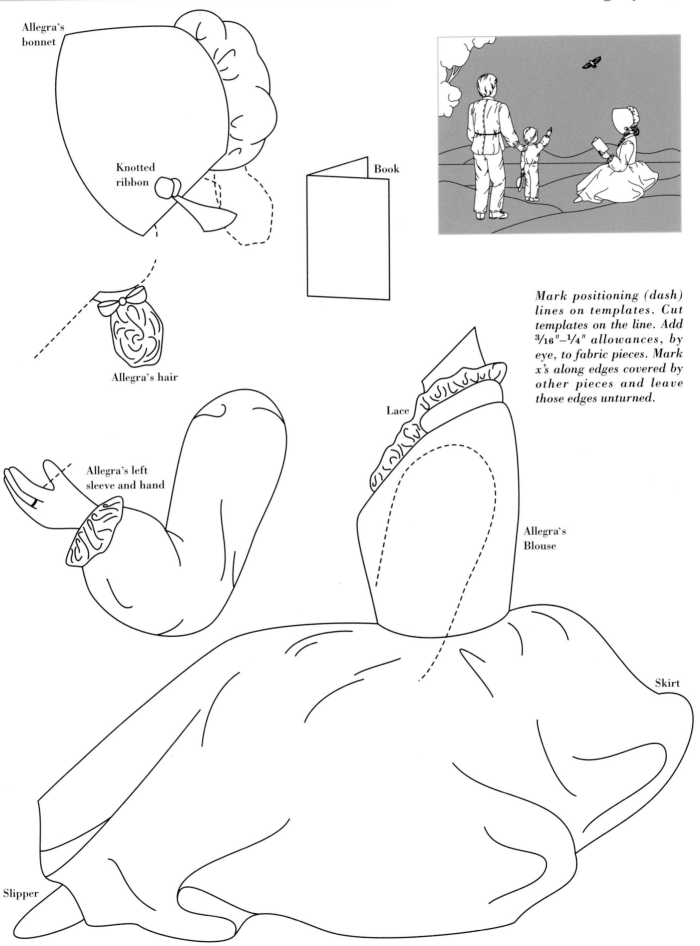

Allegra's bonnet

Knotted ribbon

Book

Allegra's hair

Mark positioning (dash) lines on templates. Cut templates on the line. Add 3/16"–1/4" allowances, by eye, to fabric pieces. Mark x's along edges covered by other pieces and leave those edges unturned.

Allegra's left sleeve and hand

Lace

Allegra's Blouse

Skirt

Slipper

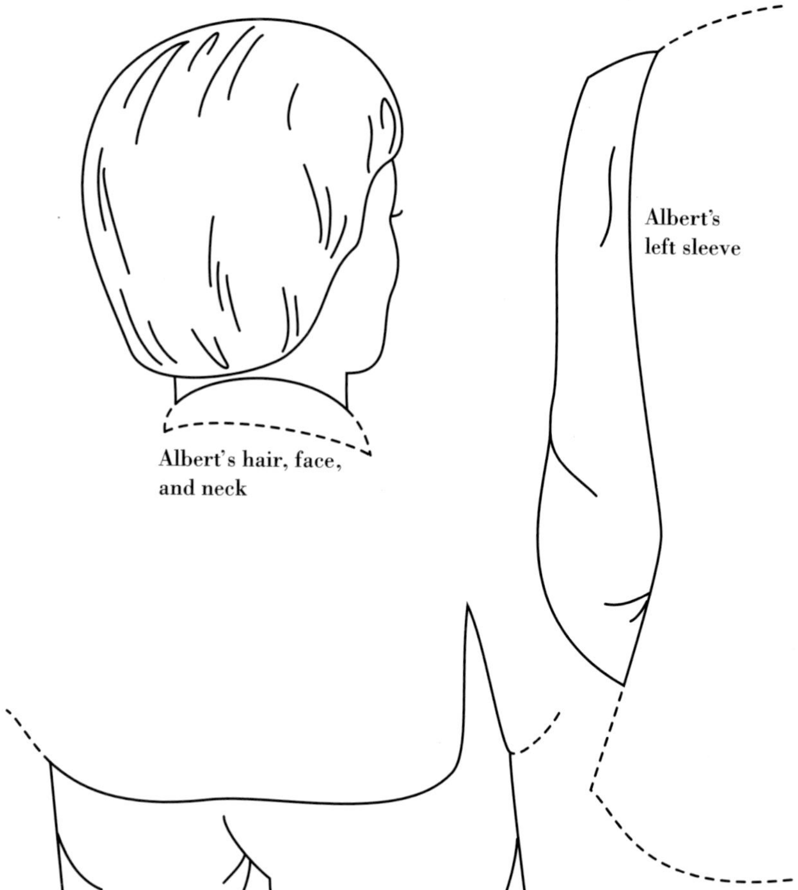

Albert's hair, face,
and neck

Albert's
left sleeve

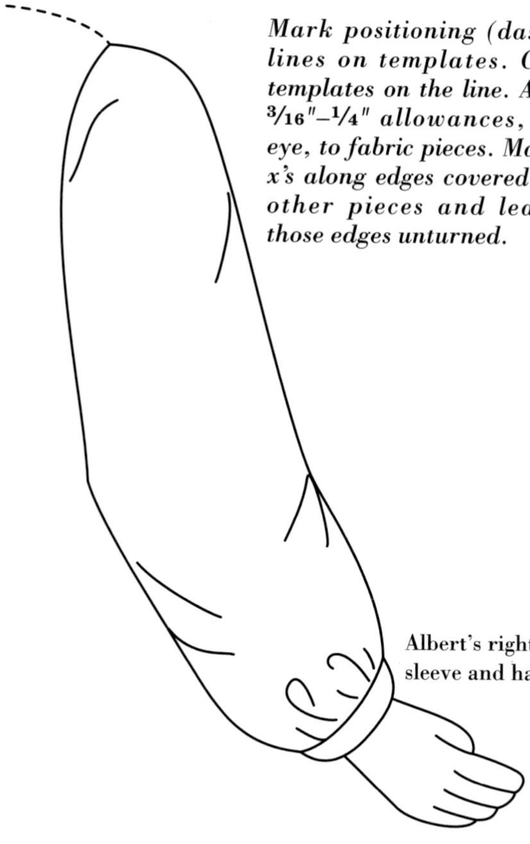

*Mark positioning (dash)
lines on templates. Cut
templates on the line. Add
³/₁₆"–¹/₄" allowances, by
eye, to fabric pieces. Mark
x's along edges covered by
other pieces and leave
those edges unturned.*

Albert's right
sleeve and hand

Albert's
trousers

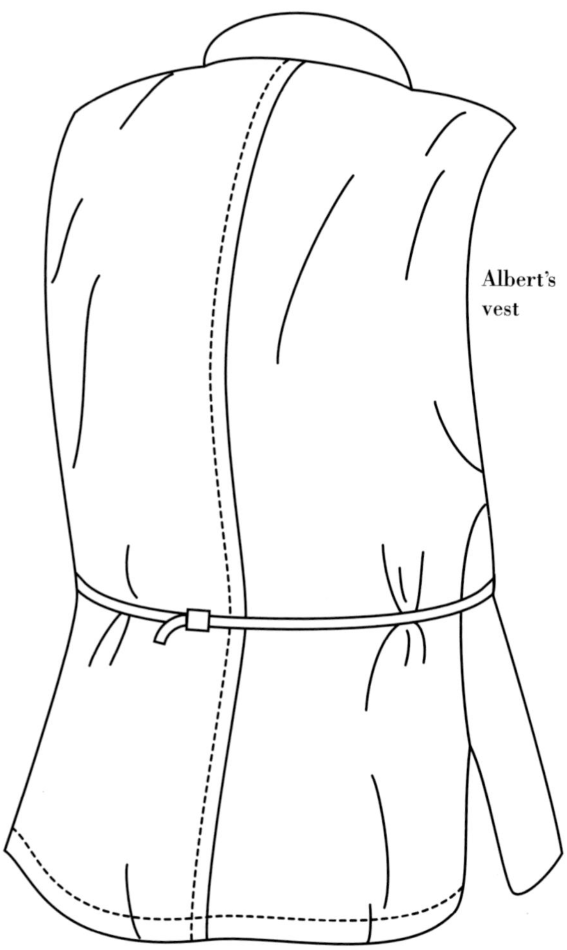

Albert's
vest

shoes

Aaron's hair, face, and neck

Branch

Tree foliage extends over top and left edges of quilt block

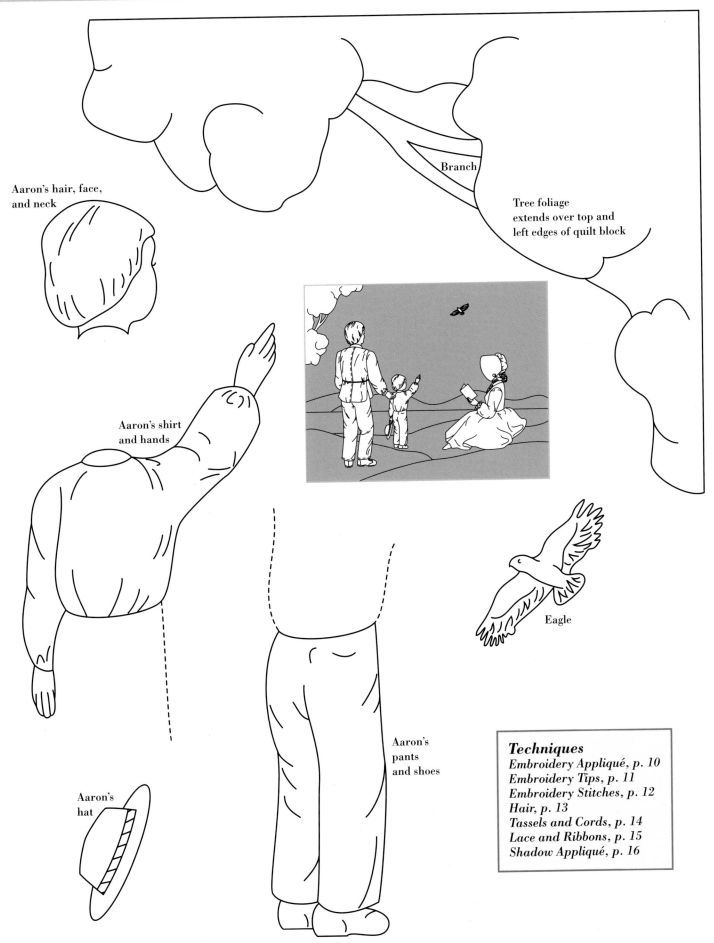

Aaron's shirt and hands

Eagle

Aaron's pants and shoes

Aaron's hat

Techniques
Embroidery Appliqué, p. 10
Embroidery Tips, p. 11
Embroidery Stitches, p. 12
Hair, p. 13
Tassels and Cords, p. 14
Lace and Ribbons, p. 15
Shadow Appliqué, p. 16

Eudora

Morning on the farm...Eudora has just completed her first chore of the day, but not everyone is happy about it. Sissie is sure she is being chased by a chicken.

Print and solid fabrics were chosen for Eudora's dress and apron that would provide a suitable background for Sissie's off-white dress. Eudora's bonnet is tied with lace seam binding.

You may want to carry the farm setting further by adding a barn in the background. Borrow figures, male, female, or child, and add a tree, clothesline, or dog from another pattern. Look at the prop pages for a cat, duck, or fence. Make a small sketch using the "X" method (page 23) and let your imagination take over.

Fabric Requirements

Small patterns (as given): Use scraps for appliqué and embellishments. Block finishes 9½" x 14". Cut background, backing, batting 11" x 15½".

Enlarged patterns (155%): Use fabric measurements below. Block finishes 14¼" x 21¼". Cut background, backing, batting 15½" x 22½".

Figure	Fabric
Faces and hands	3" x 5"
Eudora	
Dress – skirt neck and sleeves	9" x 10"
Bonnet	5" x 5"
Apron and sash	9" x 10"
Hair	2" x 2"
Sissie	
Dress	8" x 5"
Cap	3" x 3"
Slippers	2" x 2"
Props	
Chicken	3" x 4"
Basket	3" x 4"
Eggs	2" x 3"

Embroidery
Basket handle
Sissie's hair
Chicken's face

Embellishments
18" of lace seam binding for
   Eudora's bonnet
8" of ⅛" ribbon for Sissie's bonnet

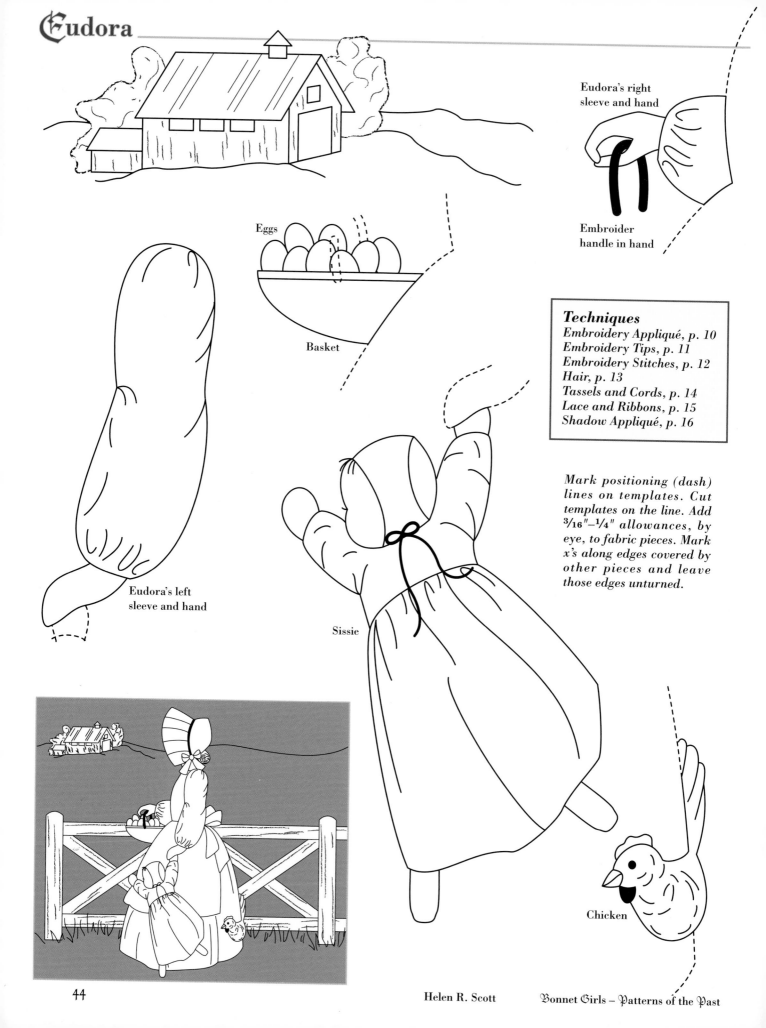

Eudora's right
sleeve and hand

Embroider
handle in hand

Eggs

Basket

Eudora's left
sleeve and hand

Sissie

Techniques
Embroidery Appliqué, p. 10
Embroidery Tips, p. 11
Embroidery Stitches, p. 12
Hair, p. 13
Tassels and Cords, p. 14
Lace and Ribbons, p. 15
Shadow Appliqué, p. 16

*Mark positioning (dash)
lines on templates. Cut
templates on the line. Add
3/16"–1/4" allowances, by
eye, to fabric pieces. Mark
x's along edges covered by
other pieces and leave
those edges unturned.*

Chicken

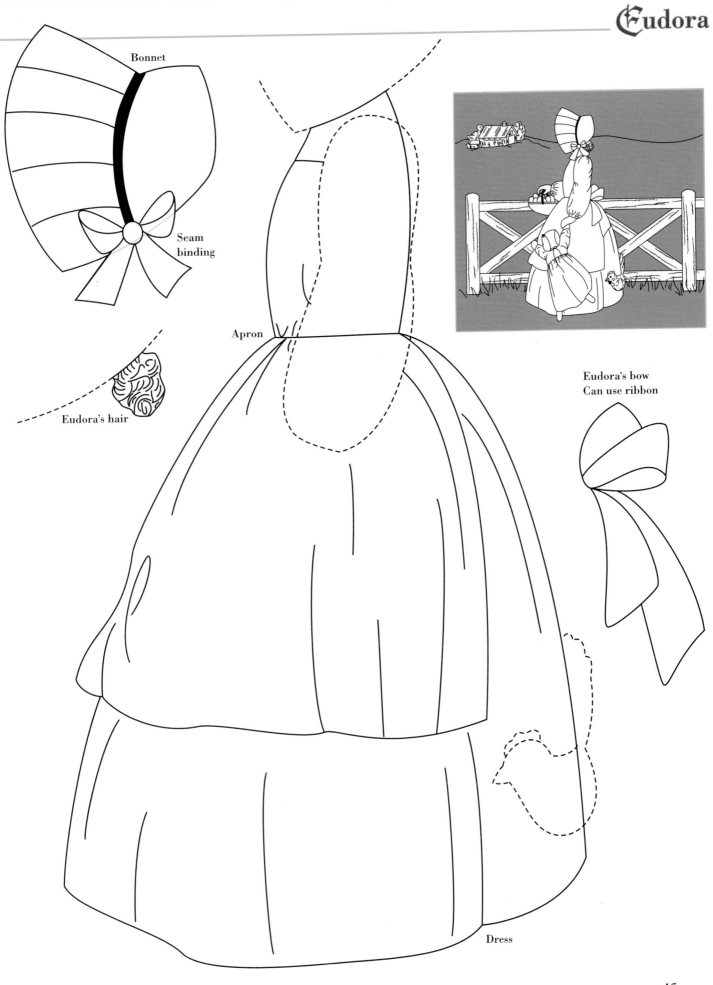

Bonnet

Seam
binding

Eudora's hair

Apron

Eudora's bow
Can use ribbon

Dress

Gwen

Gwen has her lace-trimmed parasol and is ready for a stroll. This pattern gives you an opportunity to combine your favorite solids and prints. Each gore can be a different color or print. If you choose, gores 1, 2, and 3 can be omitted completely for a plain skirt with a contrasting back panel. To make the whole dress from one fabric, leave off gores 1, 2, and 3. Attach gore 4 to the skirt pattern and cut both parts as one piece from the fabric.

Lace, ribbons, and metallic floss can be used to embellish Gwen and her parasol. If you prefer, instead of a parasol, you can give Gwen a quilt to hold, or one of the children or animals from another pattern can become her center of interest. Use your imagination, your ideas, to make many different-looking blocks from one pattern.

Fabric Requirements

Small patterns (as given): Use scraps for appliqué and embellishments. Block finishes 9½" x 14". Cut background, backing, batting 11" x 15½".

Enlarged patterns (155%): Use fabric measurements below. Block finishes 14¼" x 21¼". Cut background, backing, batting 15½" x 22½".

Figure   Fabric

Gwen

Figure	Fabric
Skirt, bodice, and sleeves	11" x 14"
Gores 1, 2, 3, and 4	10" x 10"
Bonnet, belt, gloves, and parasol	8" x 8"
Hair	2" x 2"

Embroidery
Umbrella handle and point

Embellishments
4" of 1" lace for umbrella
8" of ½" lace collar, cuffs
12" of ¼" ribbon for bonnet

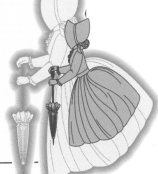

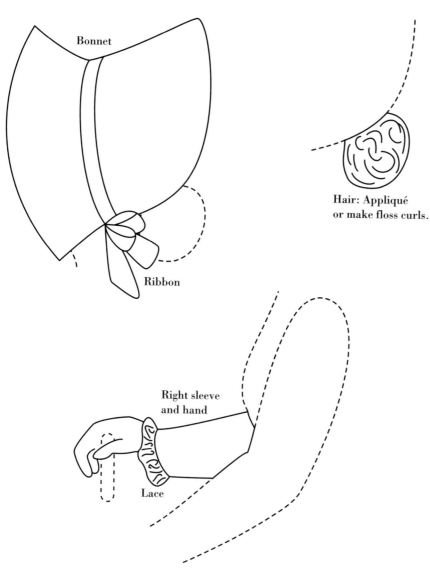

Bonnet

Hair: Appliqué
or make floss curls.

Ribbon

Right sleeve
and hand

Lace

Embroider
handle

Lace

Parasol

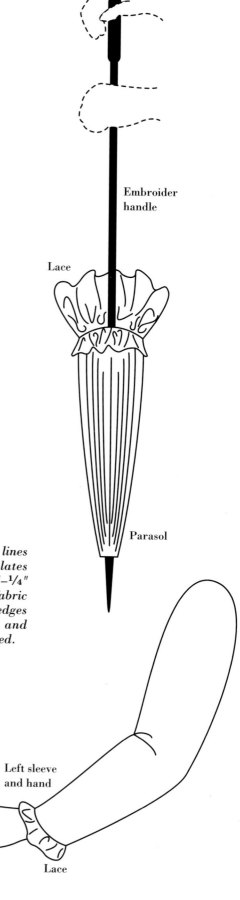

*Mark positioning (dash) lines
on templates. Cut templates
on the line. Add ³/₁₆″–¹/₄″
allowances, by eye, to fabric
pieces. Mark x's along edges
covered by other pieces and
leave those edges unturned.*

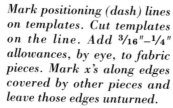

Left sleeve
and hand

Lace

Helen R. Scott   Bonnet Girls – Patterns of the Past

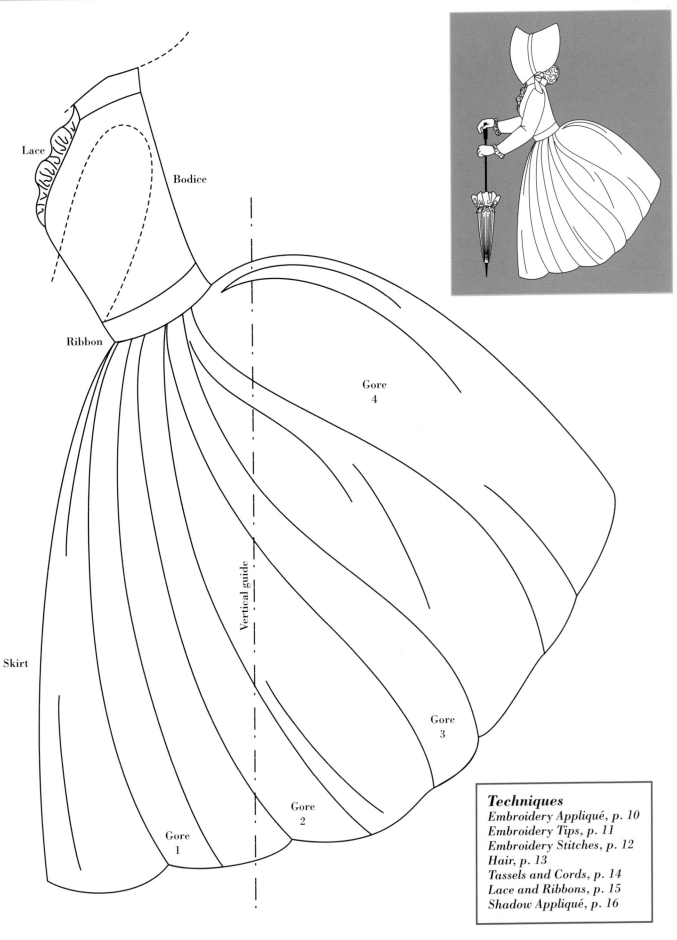

Lace

Bodice

Ribbon

Skirt

Vertical guide

Gore
4

Gore
3

Gore
2

Gore
1

Techniques
Embroidery Appliqué, p. 10
Embroidery Tips, p. 11
Embroidery Stitches, p. 12
Hair, p. 13
Tassels and Cords, p. 14
Lace and Ribbons, p. 15
Shadow Appliqué, p. 16

ħannah

This is the second pattern in which hills and a river are used as a backdrop. The block could be joined with Allegra's block to make a continuous scene. As in Allegra's block, shadow appliqué forms the hills and sky. Change the season by changing the foliage to golds, reds, and pumpkins for autumn, or use blossoms, tulips, and butterflies for spring.

The hair for both Hannah and Priscilla was cut from an animal-print fabric. Hannah's braid was made from four shades of brown floss to match the lights and darks in the hair fabric.

Fabric Requirements

Small patterns (as given): Use scraps for appliqué and embellishments. Block finishes 14" x 19". Cut background, backing, batting 15½" x 20½".

Enlarged patterns (155%): Use fabric measurements below. Block finishes 21¼" x 28½". Cut background, backing, batting 22½" x 30".

Figure	Fabric	Shadow fabric	
All faces and hands	4" x 5"	Sky	12" x 18"
		Water	5" x 20"
Hannah		Hills	4" x 18"
Blouse	6" x 6"	Grass	8" x 8"
Skirt	10" x 11"		
Hair	4" x 4"	*Embroidery*	
Baby	2" scraps	Eyes	
		Flowers	
Priscilla		Basket handle	
Dress	6" x 8"		
Hair	4" x 4"	*Embellishments*	
		Fabric paint for water reflections	
Props		Eight 8" lengths of floss for hair	
Tree foliage	11" x 14"		
Branches	8" x 18"		
Basket	3" x 3"		

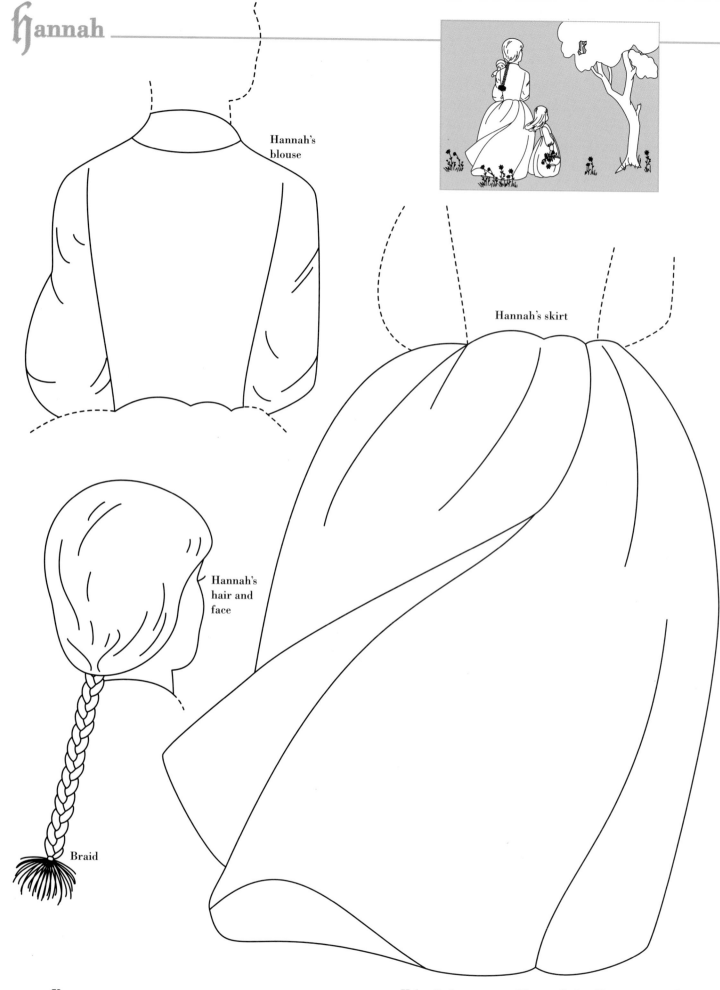

Hannah's blouse

Hannah's skirt

Hannah's hair and face

Braid

Helen R. Scott   Bonnet Girls – Patterns of the Past

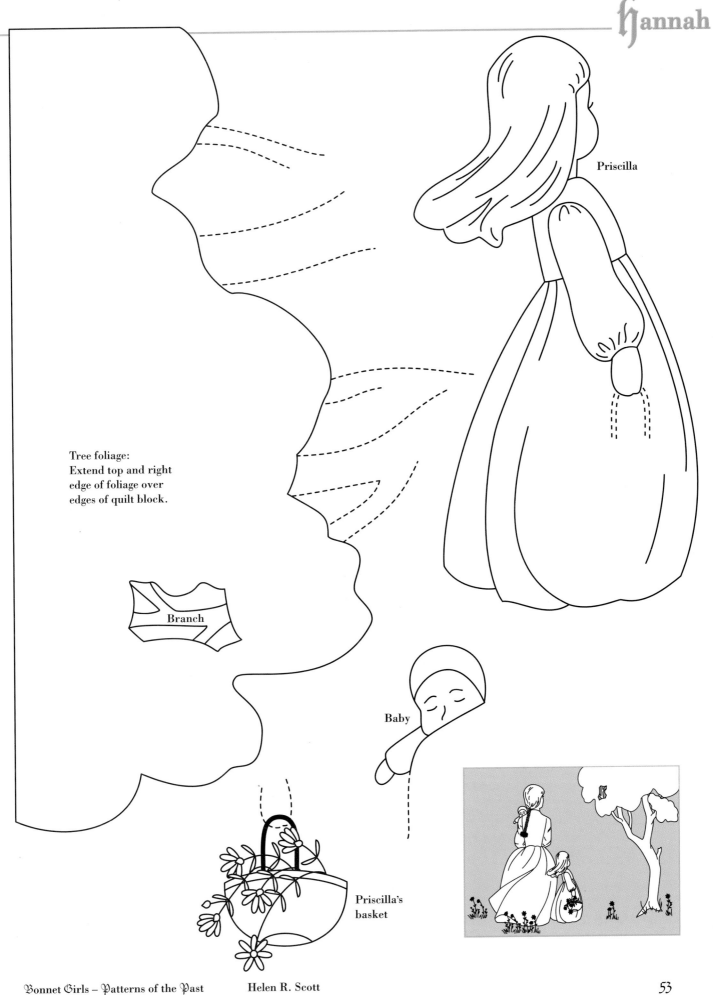

Priscilla

Tree foliage:
Extend top and right
edge of foliage over
edges of quilt block.

Branch

Baby

Priscilla's
basket

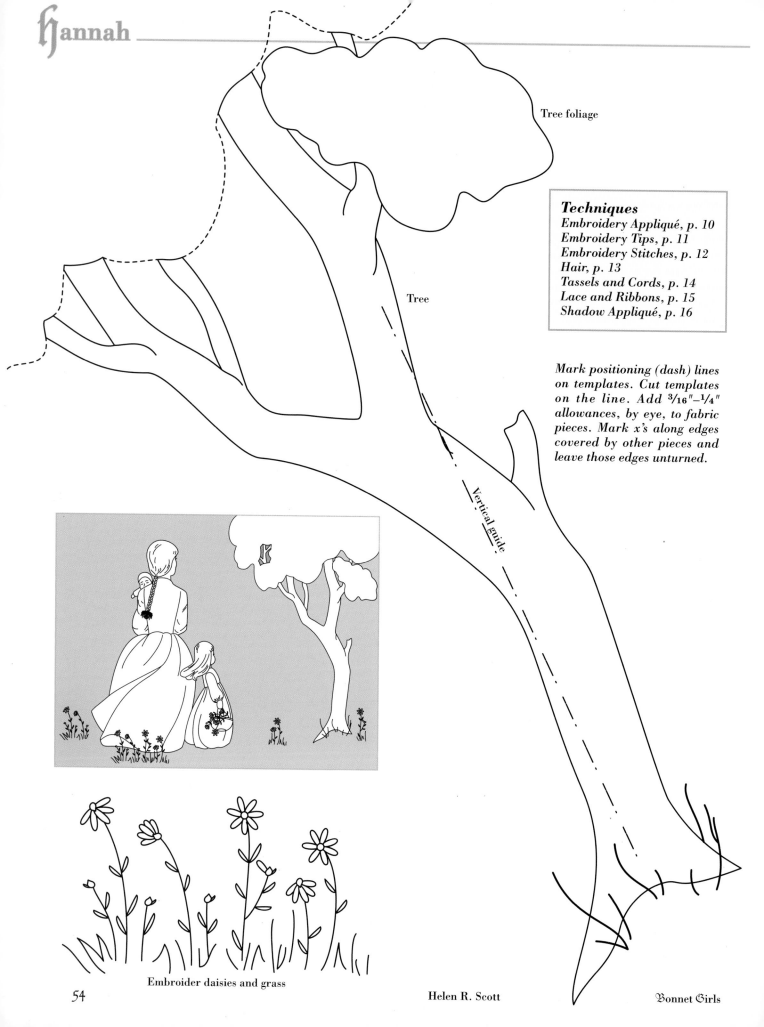

Tree foliage

Tree

Techniques
Embroidery Appliqué, p. 10
Embroidery Tips, p. 11
Embroidery Stitches, p. 12
Hair, p. 13
Tassels and Cords, p. 14
Lace and Ribbons, p. 15
Shadow Appliqué, p. 16

Mark positioning (dash) lines on templates. Cut templates on the line. Add 3/16"–1/4" allowances, by eye, to fabric pieces. Mark x's along edges covered by other pieces and leave those edges unturned.

Vertical guide

Embroider daisies and grass

Helen R. Scott

Bonnet Girls

Christmas Gift

Vibrant sounds of Christmas bells
Pierce the winter's night,
Calling all to turn their hearts
to his manger.
   He is born...
     He is born!
Christmas bells are calling,
The Christ Child is born.

Isabella

Fabric Requirements

Small patterns (as given): Use scraps for appliqué and embellishments. Block finishes 9½" x 14". Cut background, backing, batting 11" x 15½".

Enlarged patterns (155%): Use fabric measurements below. Block finishes 14¼" x 21¼". Cut background, backing, batting 15½" x 22½".

Figure	Fabric
Isabella	
Robe	7" x 16"
Skirt	7" x 11"
Hair	3" x 4"
Bonnet	4" x 4"
Hands and neck	4" x 5"
Janette	
Dress	7" x 8"
Hair	3" x 3"
Tree	9" x 18"

Embroidery
Isabella's dress (red and metallic floss)
Fringe
Knotted cord
Candles and candle holders
Star

Embellishments
Eight 9" lengths for braid
5" of ½" lace for Janette's collar
   and pantaloons
½" lace for rosettes
Heavy lace for ornaments

Isabella – The red robe is flecked with gold and trimmed with shining embroidery stitches. Along the inside edge, from neck to floor, are woven running stitches in gold metallic floss, and next to that, a row of red rayon floss outline stitches. The bottom edge of her skirt is also double stitched with a row each of red and dark red outline stitches in two strands of floss.

Combine one strand of red and one of dark red in the needle for the straight-stitch fringe. The knotted cord belt at her waist can be purchased or made from the rayon and metallic floss used to edge her robe. Sew ribbon on the bonnet.

Janette – Use ½" gathered lace for Janette's collar and pantaloons. Stitch the doll under her right hand. For the braid, use two or three shades of floss that closely match her hair fabric. Tie a ribbon close to her head and tack it in place through the bow.

Christmas tree – The tree's green-on-green fabric did not require many ornaments. A solid green would allow space for more varied ornaments and candles. Embroider candles with light yellow side-by-side outline or satin stitches. The flames are bright orange outlined with bright yellow rayon floss. Bright yellow fabric circles were basted behind the candles and the star on the wrong side of the background fabric for shadow appliqué. After the circles were outline quilted, the stitches were woven with one strand of light yellow rayon floss. The candle holders are done in gold metallic floss lazy-daisy stitches, joined at the bottom with a French knot. The tinsel can be made from gold metallic floss, chain stitches, gold rickrack, cord, or beads.

To make the rosettes, run gathering stitches along the lower edge of a 4" length of ½" lace. Pull the stitches to form the rosette. Add three or four small stitches in the center and leave several lengths of floss to form a tassel. Cut medallions or flower shapes from heavy lace for ornaments. You can purchase a star for the tree top or satin stitch it with metallic floss.

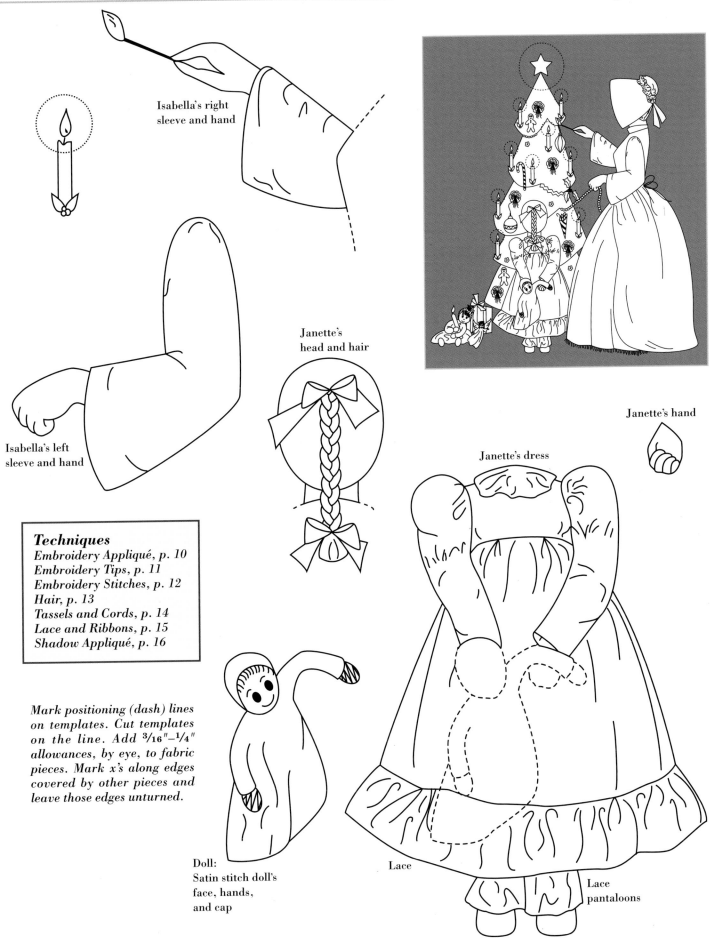

Isabella's right
sleeve and hand

Isabella's left
sleeve and hand

Janette's
head and hair

Janette's hand

Janette's dress

Techniques
Embroidery Appliqué, p. 10
Embroidery Tips, p. 11
Embroidery Stitches, p. 12
Hair, p. 13
Tassels and Cords, p. 14
Lace and Ribbons, p. 15
Shadow Appliqué, p. 16

Mark positioning (dash) lines
on templates. Cut templates
on the line. Add ³⁄₁₆"–¹⁄₄"
allowances, by eye, to fabric
pieces. Mark x's along edges
covered by other pieces and
leave those edges unturned.

Doll:
Satin stitch doll's
face, hands,
and cap

Lace

Lace
pantaloons

Isabella

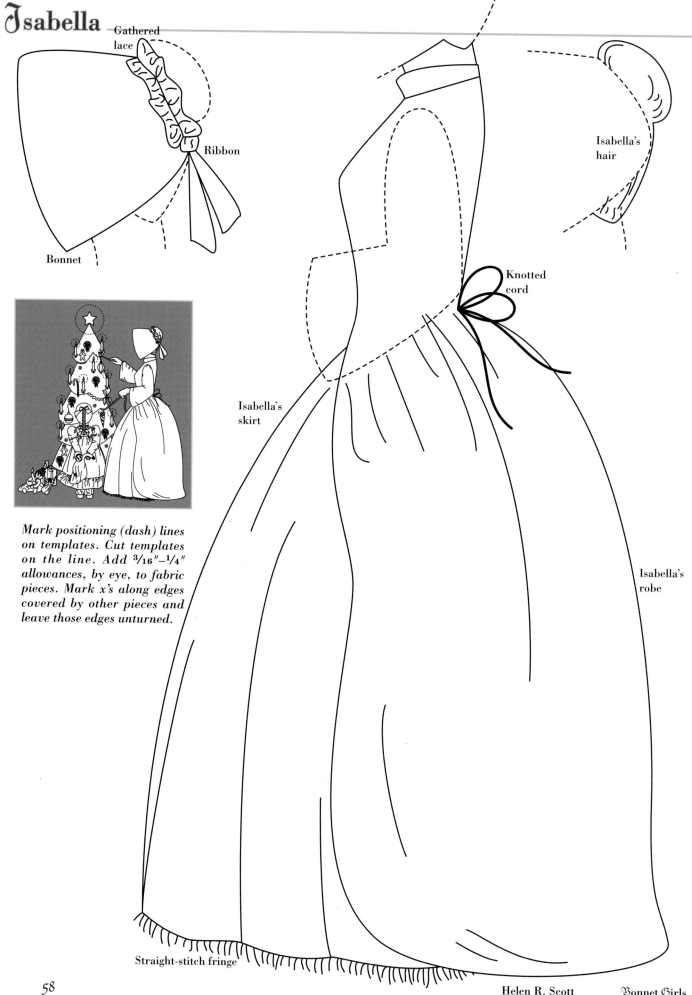

Gathered lace

Ribbon

Bonnet

Isabella's hair

Knotted cord

Isabella's skirt

Isabella's robe

Mark positioning (dash) lines on templates. Cut templates on the line. Add ³⁄₁₆"–¹⁄₄" allowances, by eye, to fabric pieces. Mark x's along edges covered by other pieces and leave those edges unturned.

Straight-stitch fringe

Helen R. Scott   Bonnet Girls

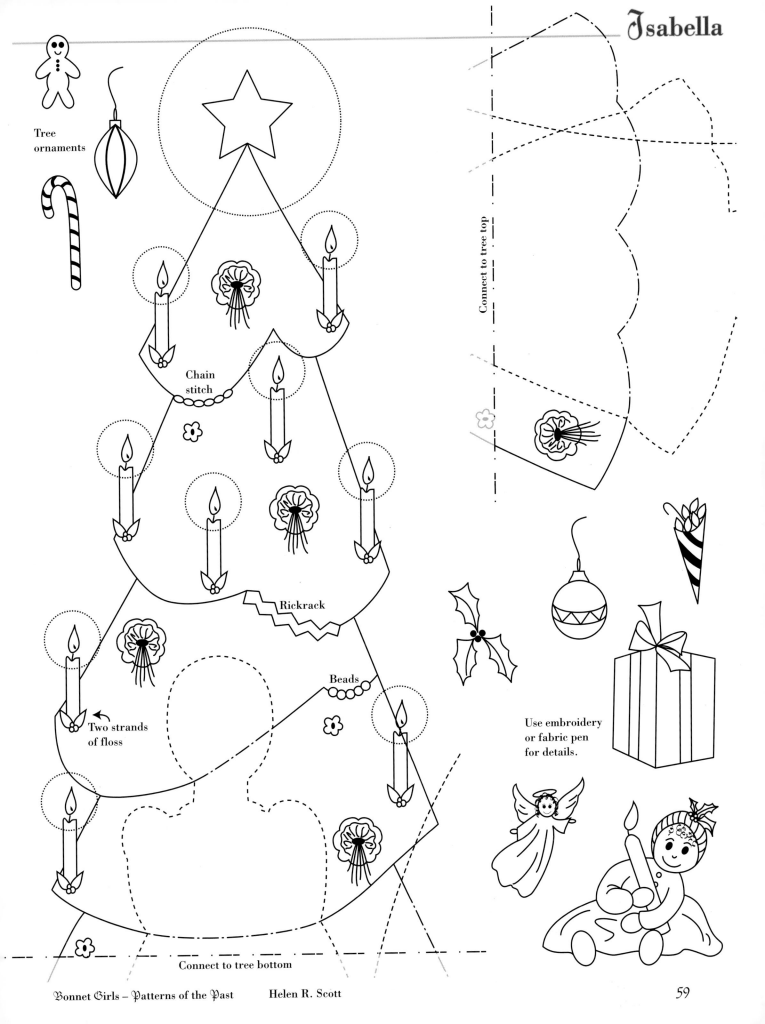

Tree
ornaments

Connect to tree top

Chain
stitch

Rickrack

Beads

Two strands
of floss

Use embroidery
or fabric pen
for details.

Connect to tree bottom

Miss Janet

Helen R. Scott · Bonnet Girls – Patterns of the Past

Katherine and William are back in school and paying close attention to Miss Janet and their arithmetic lesson.

As in many of the Bonnet Girl blocks, animal prints were used for hair. Katherine's braid combines two shades of floss to match the colors in her hair. Attach the braid under the fabric hair by threading one strand of each of the two colors in the needle and making straight stitches from fabric to braid. Tuck the end of the right braid behind the shoulder.

The buttons on Miss Janet's blouse can be purchased by the yard. Sew them in place with floss stitches between each button that match the blouse.

Printed fabric provides the alphabet on top of the chalkboard, but a permanent marker could be used to make the alphabet. Use fabric, embroidery, or acrylic paint for creating the math or your favorite subject on the chalkboard.

Fabric Requirements

Small patterns (as given): Use scraps for appliqué and embellishments. Block finishes 9½" x 14". Cut background, backing, batting 11" x 15½".

Enlarged patterns (155%): Use fabric measurements below. Block finishes 14¼" x 21¼". Cut background, backing, batting 15½" x 22½".

Figure	Fabric
Miss Janet	
Skirt	8" x 11"
Blouse	6" x 7"
Hair	3" x 3"
Bonnet	5" x 5"
Hands	3" x 3"
Katherine	
Dress	6" x 8"
Apron	6" x 8"
Hair	3" x 3"
Shoes and neck	scraps
William	
Pants	4" x 5"
Shirt	4" x 5"
Hair	3" x 3"
Shoes, hand, and leg	2" x 2"
Stockings	2" x 3"

Props
Chalkboard	8" x 9"
Books	scraps

Embroidery
Pencils
Math

Embellishments
18" of ⅝" ribbon for Janet's sash and cuffs
10" of ⅜" ribbon for Katherine's sash
10" of ½" lace for Katherine's apron
9" of ¼" lace for Janet's bonnet
6" of ¼" ribbon for Janet's neckline
3½" string beads for Janet's bodice
Five 7" lengths of floss for Katherine's 5" braid

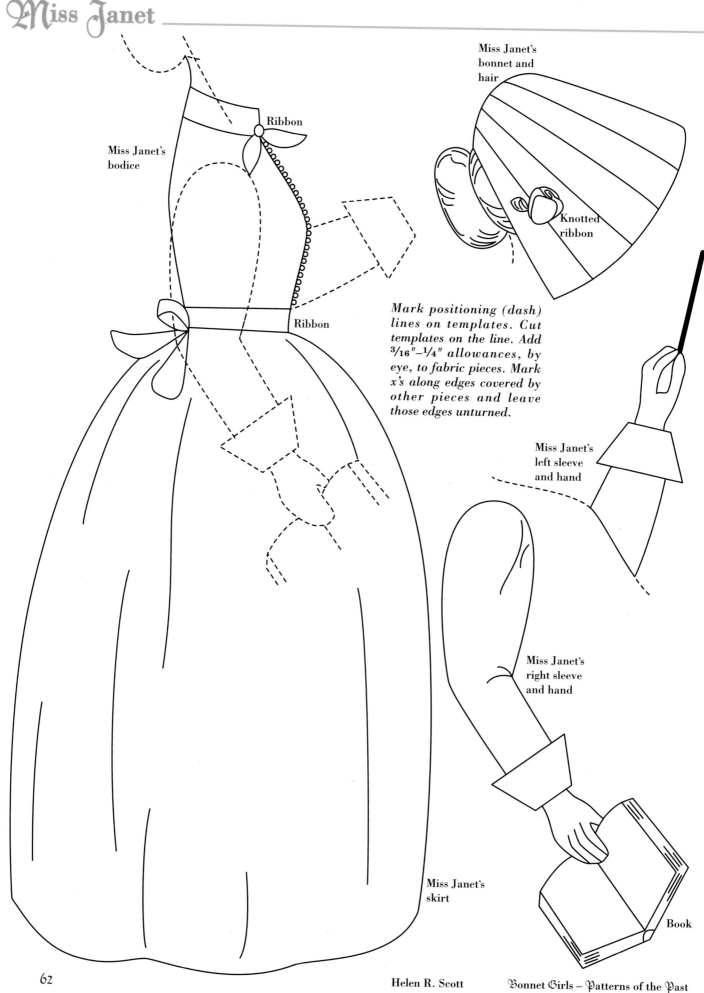

Miss Janet's bonnet and hair

Miss Janet's bodice

Ribbon

Knotted ribbon

Ribbon

Mark positioning (dash) lines on templates. Cut templates on the line. Add 3/16"–1/4" allowances, by eye, to fabric pieces. Mark x's along edges covered by other pieces and leave those edges unturned.

Miss Janet's left sleeve and hand

Miss Janet's right sleeve and hand

Miss Janet's skirt

Book

Helen R. Scott   Bonnet Girls – Patterns of the Past

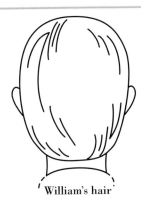

William's hair

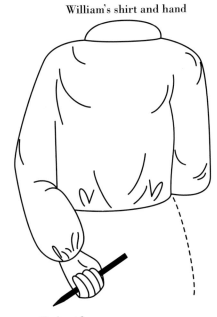

William's shirt and hand

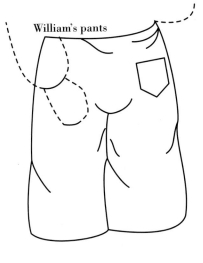

William's pants

Embroider pencil

Techniques

Embroidery Appliqué, p. 10
Embroidery Tips, p. 11
Embroidery Stitches, p. 12
Hair, p. 13
Tassels and Cords, p. 14
Lace and Ribbons, p. 15
Shadow Appliqué, p. 16

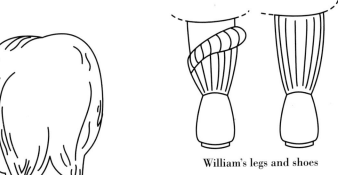

William's legs and shoes

Book

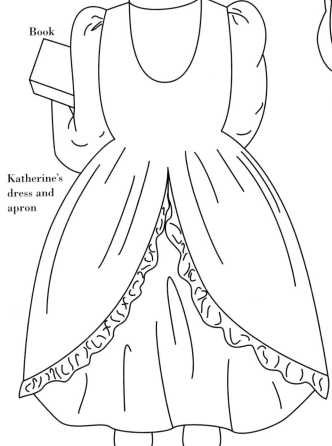

Katherine's dress and apron

Shoes

Katherine's hair and face

Ribbon

Karen

July Fourth
Sparklers
fire crackers
apple pie and picnics.
High blue skies
hot summer nights and
sudden summer storms.
Parades
our grand old flag and
Irving Berlin.
GOD BLESS AMERICA!

Karen and Luke are dressed in red, white, and blue to celebrate the Fourth. Find your reddest red, bluest blue, and most sparkling white for this block. Stars and stripes would be perfect.

Karen's blouse needs a special sleeve pattern if striped fabric is used. Refer to the pattern labeled "stripes." Make tucks in the fabric as indicated. Printed dog fabric was used for her hair and for Skipper, the cautious dog. Trim Karen's bonnet with narrow lace and knotted ½" seam binding. Use narrow ribbon at her waist and knotted ribbon on Luke's hat.

Embroider Luke's flag and firecracker with side-by-side outline stitches. Silver embroidery floss gives sparkle to Karen's sparklers.

Bright orange and yellow fabric was used for the shadow-appliquéd burst of distant fire crackers and the light from Karen's sparkler. You may want to appliqué, embroider, or paint these embellishments. Various sizes of stars were quilted with rayon floss on the background.

Fabric Requirements

Small patterns (as given): Use scraps for appliqué and embellishments. Block finishes 9½" x 14". Cut background, backing, batting 11" x 15½".

Enlarged patterns (155%): Use fabric measurements below. Block finishes 14¼" x 21¼". Cut background, backing, batting 15½" x 22½".

Both Figures	**Fabric**
Hands	4" x 4"
Karen	
Skirt	11" x 12"
Blouse and arms	6" x 9"
Bonnet	5" x 5"
Hair	4" x 3"
Luke	
Shirt	4" x 6"
Pants	4" x 6"
Hat	4" x 4"
Dog	
Fur	3" x 4"
Other	
Shadow fabrics	scraps
Embroidery	
Sparklers	
Firecracker	
Flag	
Dog's face	

Embellishments
12" of ¾" seam binding or ribbon for
    Karen's bonnet
9" of ¼" ribbon for Karen's waist and
    Luke's hat

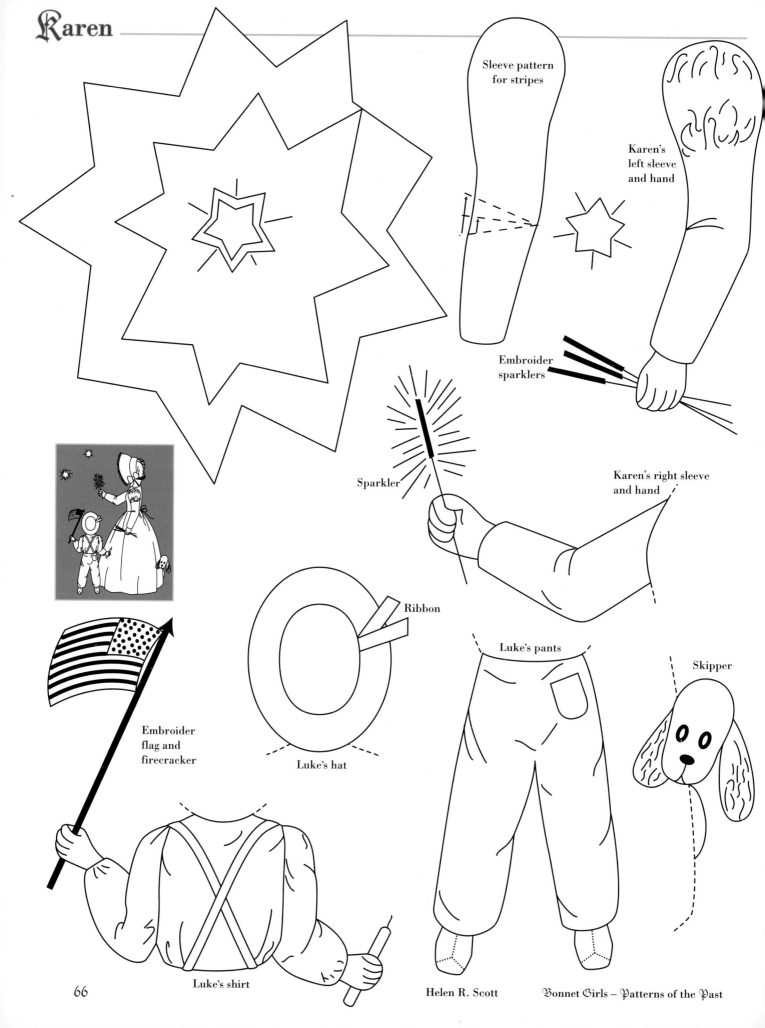

Sleeve pattern for stripes

Karen's left sleeve and hand

Embroider sparklers

Sparkler

Karen's right sleeve and hand

Ribbon

Luke's pants

Skipper

Embroider flag and firecracker

Luke's hat

Luke's shirt

Helen R. Scott   Bonnet Girls – Patterns of the Past

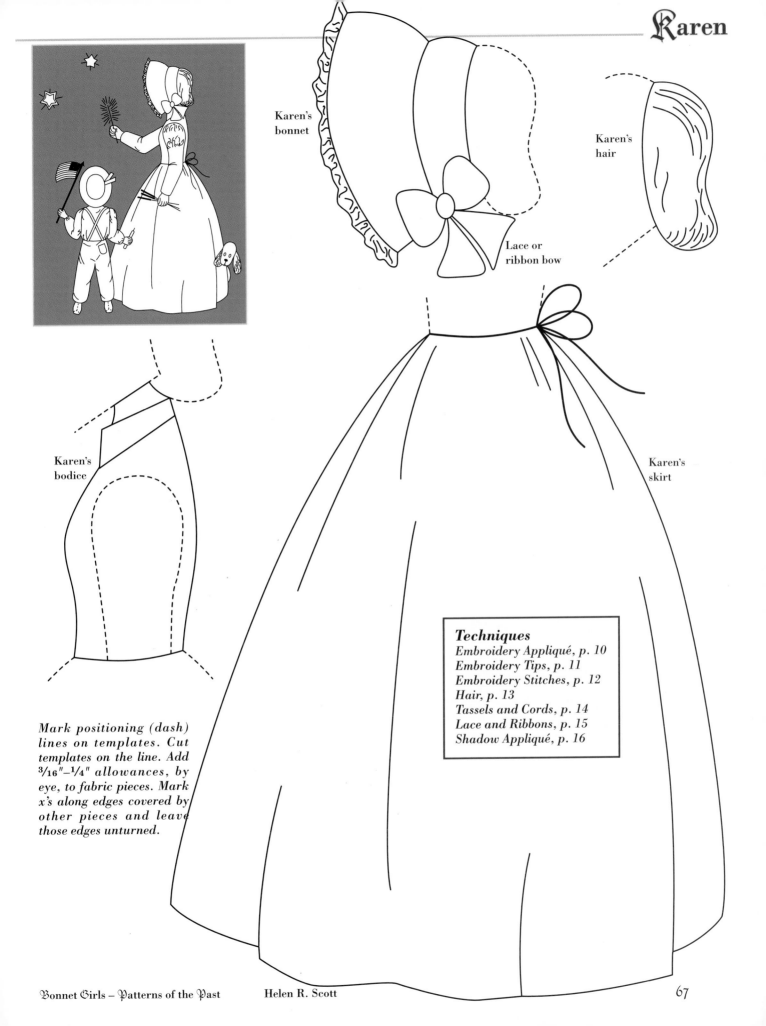

Karen's bonnet

Karen's hair

Lace or ribbon bow

Karen's bodice

Karen's skirt

Techniques
Embroidery Appliqué, p. 10
Embroidery Tips, p. 11
Embroidery Stitches, p. 12
Hair, p. 13
Tassels and Cords, p. 14
Lace and Ribbons, p. 15
Shadow Appliqué, p. 16

Mark positioning (dash) lines on templates. Cut templates on the line. Add ³⁄₁₆"–¹⁄₄" allowances, by eye, to fabric pieces. Mark x's along edges covered by other pieces and leave those edges unturned.

The Awakening
March sun brightness, sycamores-white against blue skies and dancing clouds.

Crow silhouettes ride top-most branches, calling springs approach to budding green.

Soft winds stir autumn's brown to flight revealing jonquil spears, violets, and sleeping lions.

Maureen

March winds, a sunny day. Spring is just around the corner. Maureen and Maggie are walking to meet the welcome new season. Bright yellow fabrics and a flowing scarf proclaim the windy March day and set the atmosphere for the block.

The flowers on Maureen's large hat were needle-turn appliquéd, as were the blowing petals. A ¾"-wide stretch-lace seam binding was used for her scarf and belt. It can be tied to form bows or simply knotted, and it is easily shaped to form graceful, curved streamers. Pin streamers in place and tack them along their edges with a single strand of matching floss or thread.

Woven running stitches or baby rickrack will secure the lace that edges Maureen's skirt. Scalloped woven running stitches in a rust floss to match belt, scarf, and glove pick up the color in her print dress. The large ruffle on her underskirt is formed with outline embroidery stitches.

Maggie the dog, appropriately, is cut from a much larger dog-print fabric. Cut her template from transparent plastic that can be moved about on the fabric to give her markings a natural look.

Fabric Requirements

Small patterns (as given): Use scraps for appliqué and embellishments. Block finishes 9½" x 14". Cut background, backing, batting 11" x 15½".

Enlarged patterns (155%): Use fabric measurements below. Block finishes 14¼" x 21¼". Cut background, backing, batting 15½" x 22½".

Figure	Fabric		
Maureen			
Dress	13" x 16"		
Hat and underskirt	10" x 13"	**Embroidery**	
Scarf and belt		Underskirt	
Glove	3" x 3"	Dog's face	
Maggie, the dog		**Embellishments**	
Fur	6" x 6"	18" of ⅜" gathered lace for skirt	
		18" of ¾" stretch-lace seam binding	
Prop		or ribbon for scarf and belt	
Flowers	4" x 4"	3" length of strung beads for back of bodice	

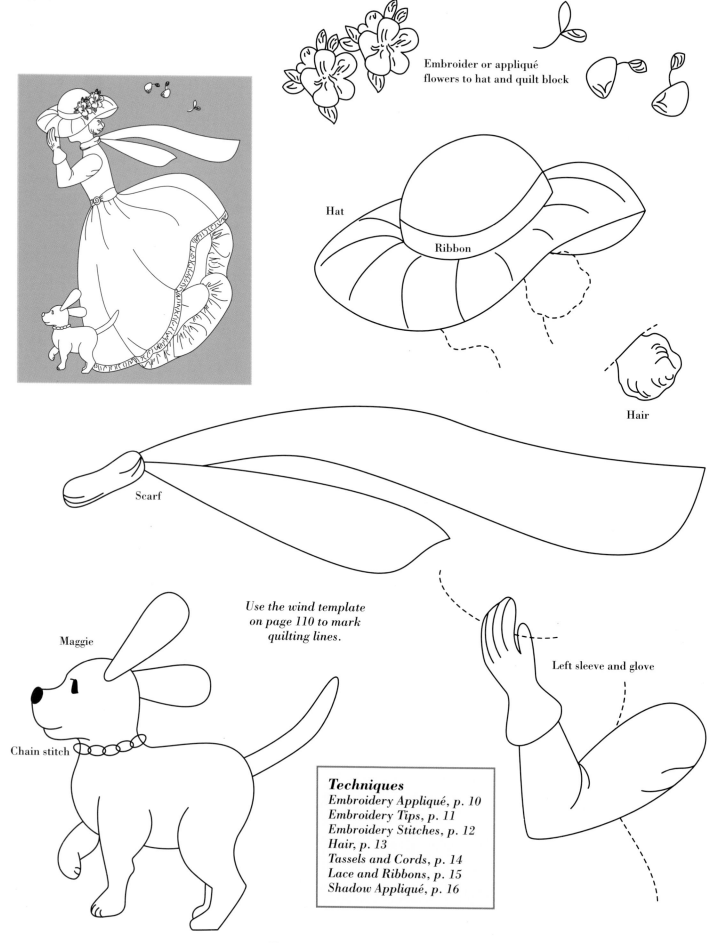

Embroider or appliqué flowers to hat and quilt block

Hat

Ribbon

Hair

Scarf

Use the wind template on page 110 to mark quilting lines.

Maggie

Chain stitch

Left sleeve and glove

Techniques
Embroidery Appliqué, p. 10
Embroidery Tips, p. 11
Embroidery Stitches, p. 12
Hair, p. 13
Tassels and Cords, p. 14
Lace and Ribbons, p. 15
Shadow Appliqué, p. 16

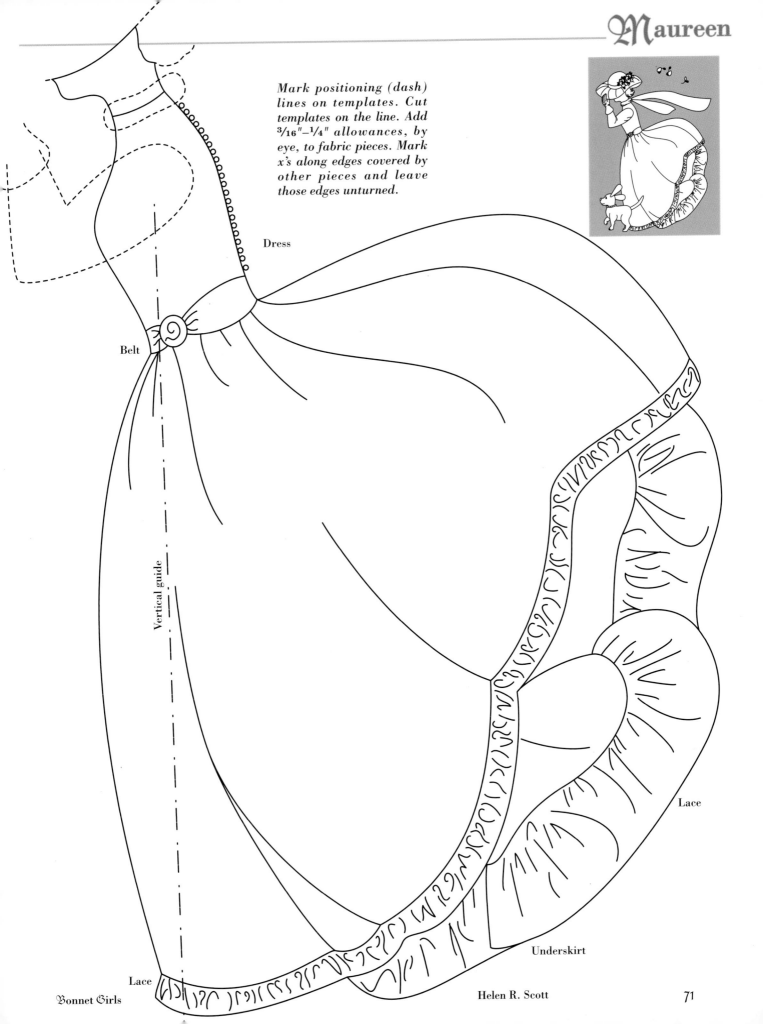

Mark positioning (dash) lines on templates. Cut templates on the line. Add ³⁄₁₆"–¹⁄₄" allowances, by eye, to fabric pieces. Mark x's along edges covered by other pieces and leave those edges unturned.

Dress

Belt

Vertical guide

Lace

Lace

Underskirt

Bonnet Girls

Helen R. Scott

71

Lois Jean

Helen R. Scott   Bonnet Girls – Patterns of the Past

Lois Jean has an errand to run, and neither storm nor snow can stop her. She wears a warm fur jacket to ward off the cold. The fur is not as difficult to make as it may seem. Look for printed animal fabrics. Those printed to make toys and decorate sweatshirts can be used for fur clothing. Trace the jacket pattern on transparent plastic, move it around until the fur appears to lie as it would grow. Appliqué with two strands of floss and varied sizes of straight stitches following the printed lines on the fabric. If the bear fabric is too dark, turn it over and use the wrong side.

Baby rickrack was used to trim the bonnet edge, and cord was knotted and couched to the bonnet. Instructions for making the cord are on page 14. The wrong side of a soft floral print was used to give the effect of snow in shadow.

The background fabric is a blend which lends itself to shadow appliqué. Dark blue fabric with small stars was used for storm clouds under the white blend block fabric. Two and three strands of white floss French knots were scattered over the entire block. They were added after the quilting was completed.

Fabric Requirements

Small patterns (as given): Use scraps for appliqué and embellishments. Block finishes 9½" x 14". Cut background, backing, batting 11" x 15½".

Enlarged patterns (155%): Use fabric measurements below. Block finishes 14¼" x 21¼". Cut background, backing, batting 15½" x 22½".

Figure	Fabric
Lois Jean	
Skirt	10" x 10"
Fur jacket	6" x 7"
Bonnet and mitten	5" x 6"
Scarf	5" x 9"
Props	
Basket	4" x 5"
Towel	3" x 5"
Left snow bank	7" x 12"
Right snow bank	7" x 9"
Other	
Shadow fabric	7" x 14"

Embroidery
Jacket
Snowflakes
Cardinal
Branch

Embellishments
5" of rickrack for bonnet
3" of cord for bonnet

Lois Jean

Fur jacket

Mittens

Bonnet

Scarf

Skirt

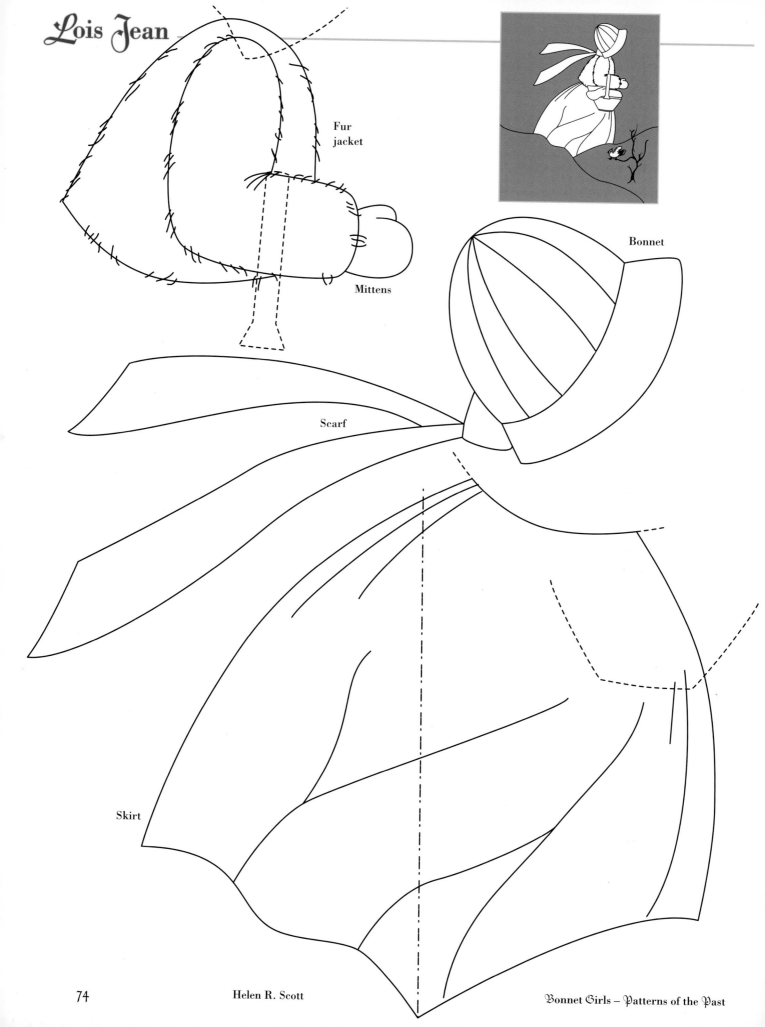

Helen R. Scott

Bonnet Girls – Patterns of the Past

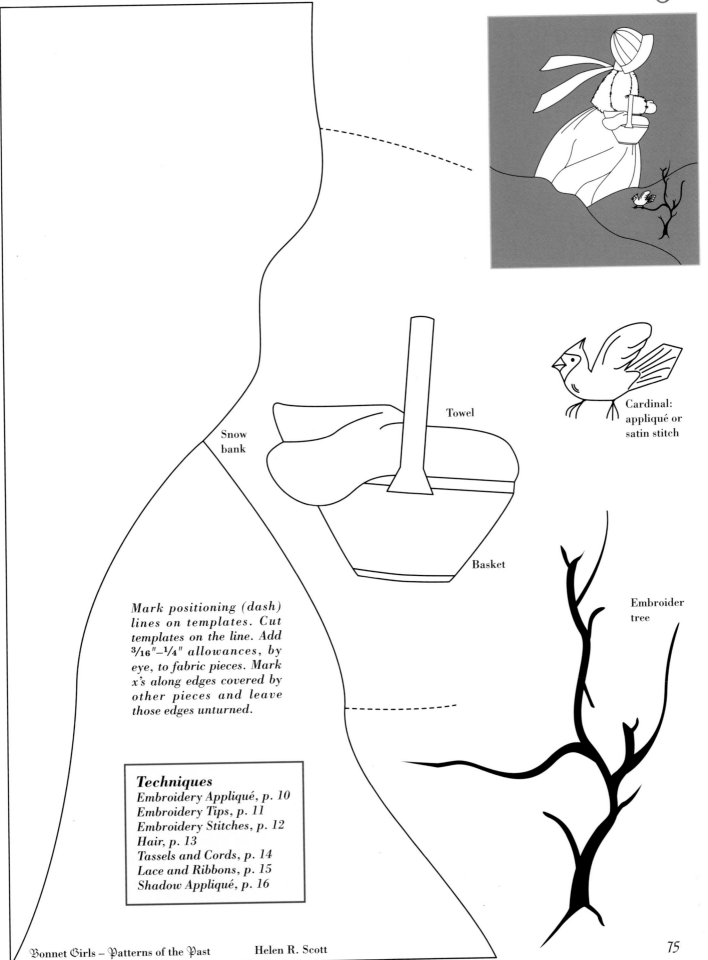

Snow
bank

Towel

Basket

Cardinal:
appliqué or
satin stitch

Embroider
tree

Mark positioning (dash) lines on templates. Cut templates on the line. Add 3/16"–1/4" allowances, by eye, to fabric pieces. Mark x's along edges covered by other pieces and leave those edges unturned.

Techniques
Embroidery Appliqué, p. 10
Embroidery Tips, p. 11
Embroidery Stitches, p. 12
Hair, p. 13
Tassels and Cords, p. 14
Lace and Ribbons, p. 15
Shadow Appliqué, p. 16

Momma

Momma's Chair
I wonder who built the rocking chair
made it soft and set it there,
so Momma could rock the baby.
I wonder who made the rockers strong
nice and curved and extra long,
so little boys could ride.
I wonder who made the back so tall,
to guard his girls from spiders small,
I know...Papa did!

Helen R. Scott   Bonnet Girls – Patterns of the Past

It's play time for Momma and baby Hayden. By lowering Momma's arm and tilting her bonnet down a little, Hayden could be standing on her lap. The baby can be dressed in a diaper and shirt or a gown, or he can be nude, just coming from a bath.

Purchased cord was used on Momma's bonnet and waist. Be aware that cord can untwist and fray, so tuck the ends under the appliqué pieces and tack through all thicknesses with matching floss or thread. I like to turn the block over and make additional stitches to hold the cord and knots in place. Bows can be cumbersome and heavy, so I used a cluster of two or three tight knots or loops instead.

The heading was removed from ½" lace, which was regathered with a running stitch and appliquéd under the edges of the skirt, bodice, and bonnet. A row of rayon floss outline stitches accent these edges.

Fabric Requirements

Small patterns (as given): Use scraps for appliqué and embellishments. Block finishes 9½" x 14". Cut background, backing, batting 11" x 15½".

Enlarged patterns (155%): Use fabric measurements below. Block finishes 14¼" x 21¼". Cut background, backing, batting 15½" x 22½".

Figure	Fabric
View 1	
Face, hands, feet	5" x 5"
Baby clothes	scraps 4" x 4"
View 2	
Nude baby, hand	5" x 7"
Momma	
Dress	10" x 14"
Sleeve and bonnet	5" x 8"
Slippers	2" x 2"
Hair	3" x 3"

Props

Chair frame	6" x 8"
Cushions	4" x 7"

Optional props

Wash cloth	2" x 2"
Basin	3" x 4"
Bear	4" x 4"

Embroidery
Baby's hair and features
Bear's face

Embellishments
View 1
16" of ½" lace for skirt, bodice, and bonnet
18" of cord or ribbon for belt and bonnet

View 2
Ten 8" lengths of floss for braid
4" beaded lace for Momma's bonnet
14" of ¼" ribbon for Momma's bonnet
   and waist
2½" of strung beads for bodice

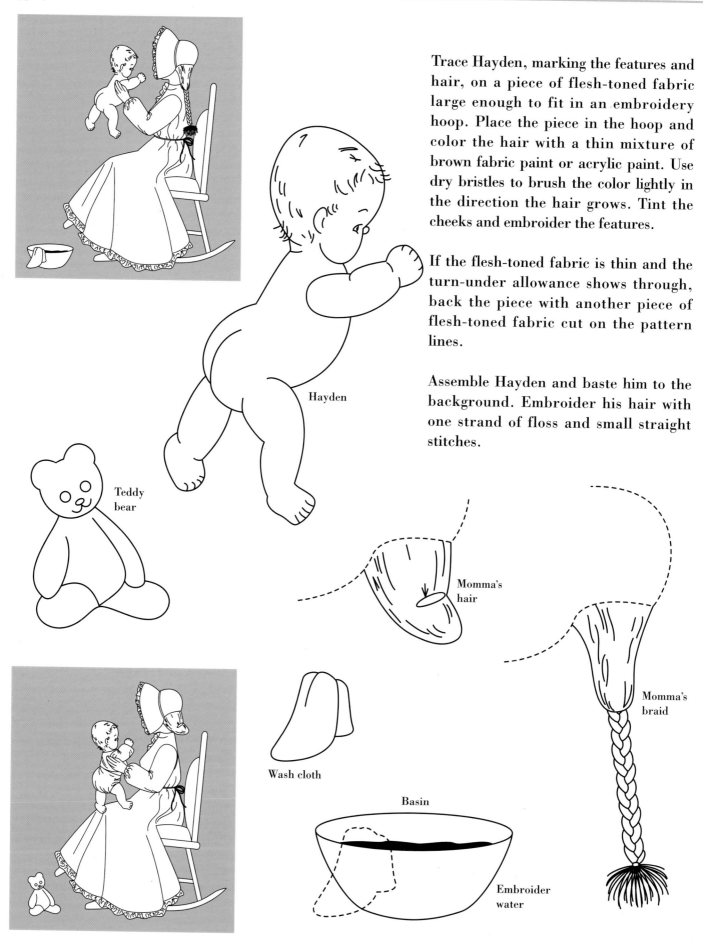

Trace Hayden, marking the features and hair, on a piece of flesh-toned fabric large enough to fit in an embroidery hoop. Place the piece in the hoop and color the hair with a thin mixture of brown fabric paint or acrylic paint. Use dry bristles to brush the color lightly in the direction the hair grows. Tint the cheeks and embroider the features.

If the flesh-toned fabric is thin and the turn-under allowance shows through, back the piece with another piece of flesh-toned fabric cut on the pattern lines.

Assemble Hayden and baste him to the background. Embroider his hair with one strand of floss and small straight stitches.

Hayden

Teddy bear

Momma's hair

Momma's braid

Wash cloth

Basin

Embroider water

Helen R. Scott   Bonnet Girls – Patterns of the Past

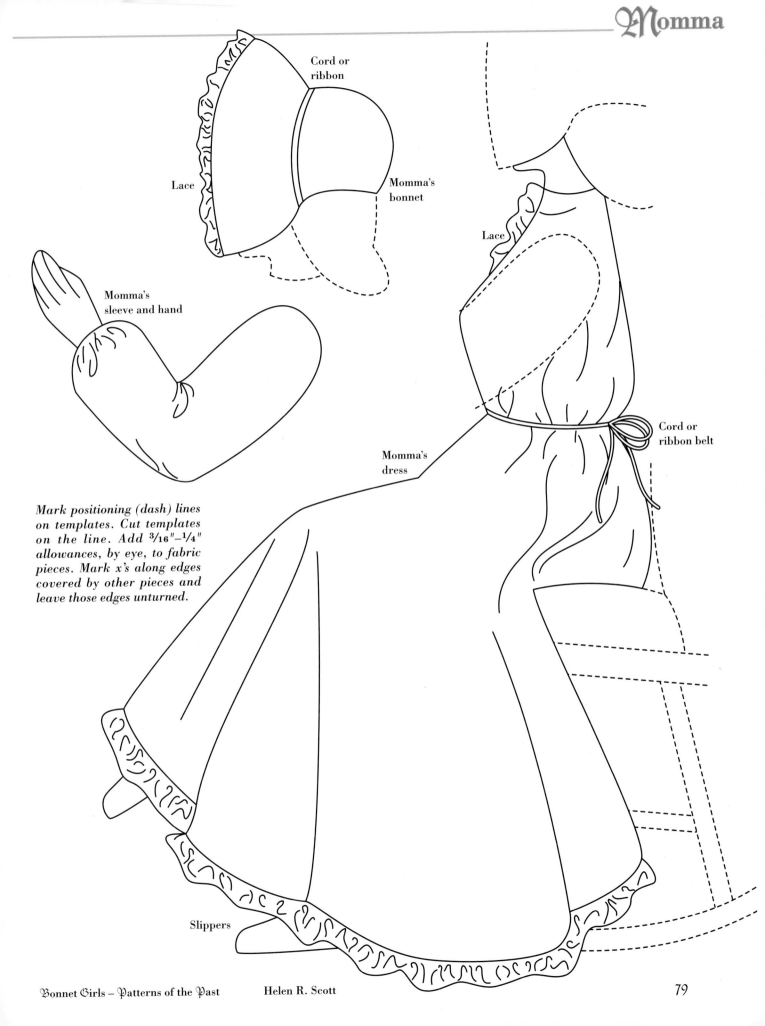

Cord or ribbon

Lace

Momma's bonnet

Lace

Momma's sleeve and hand

Momma's dress

Cord or ribbon belt

Mark positioning (dash) lines on templates. Cut templates on the line. Add ³⁄₁₆"–¹⁄₄" allowances, by eye, to fabric pieces. Mark x's along edges covered by other pieces and leave those edges unturned.

Slippers

Hayden's cap

Hayden's shirt

Techniques
Embroidery Appliqué, p. 10
Embroidery Tips, p. 11
Embroidery Stitches, p. 12
Hair, p. 13
Tassels and Cords, p. 14
Lace and Ribbons, p. 15
Shadow Appliqué, p. 16

Hayden's diaper

Hayden's gown

Mark positioning (dash) lines on templates. Cut templates on the line. Add 3/16"–1/4" allowances, by eye, to fabric pieces. Mark x's along edges covered by other pieces and leave those edges unturned.

Rocking chair

Helen R. Scott

Bonnet Girls – Patterns of the Past

Leah

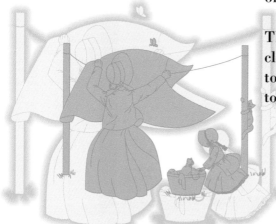

It's wash day, and Leah, who is not as fortunate as you and I who have dryers, is hanging her blanket to dry in the wind. Quilting lines drawn with the wind template create a windy-day atmosphere.

I used marbled fabric for the blanket. You may want to design and construct your own patchwork or crazy quilt to hang on the line. Trace the entire blanket outline on paper to work out your ideas and make your pattern. A floral, printed patchwork or small geometric fabric could be used for the quilt instead.

The scene could be varied by making the block wider, the clothesline longer, and by adding more items to the line. Refer to the props section for more ready-to-hang wash. Consider, too, letting other Bonnet Girls use the line for their washing.

Fabric Requirements

Small patterns (as given): Use scraps for appliqué and embellishments. Block finishes 14" x 19". Cut background, backing, batting 15½" x 20½".

Enlarged patterns (155%): Use fabric measurements below. Block finishes 21¼" x 28½". Cut background, backing, batting 22½" x 30".

Figure	Fabric
Leah	
Jacket	10" x 12"
Skirt	10" x 12"
Bonnet	5" x 5"
Bonnet band	4" x 5"
Hands	2" x 4"
Hair	1" x 1"
Katie	
Jacket	6" x 6"
Skirt and bonnet	7" x 8"
Hand	1" x 1"

Props

Blanket	12" x 18"
Post	17" x 3"
Basket	6" x 4"
Contents of basket	scraps
Cats	5" x 6"

Embroidery

Clothesline
Grass
Cat's face
Wash basket handle
Butterfly
Katie's coat buttons – French knots

Embellishments

6" of ½" lace for underskirt
10" of ¼" ribbon for Katie's bonnet
Four 8" lengths of floss for braid

Katie's bonnet and braid

Ribbon

Katie's sleeve and hand

Katie's coat and skirt

Lace

Leah's jacket

Post

Cat

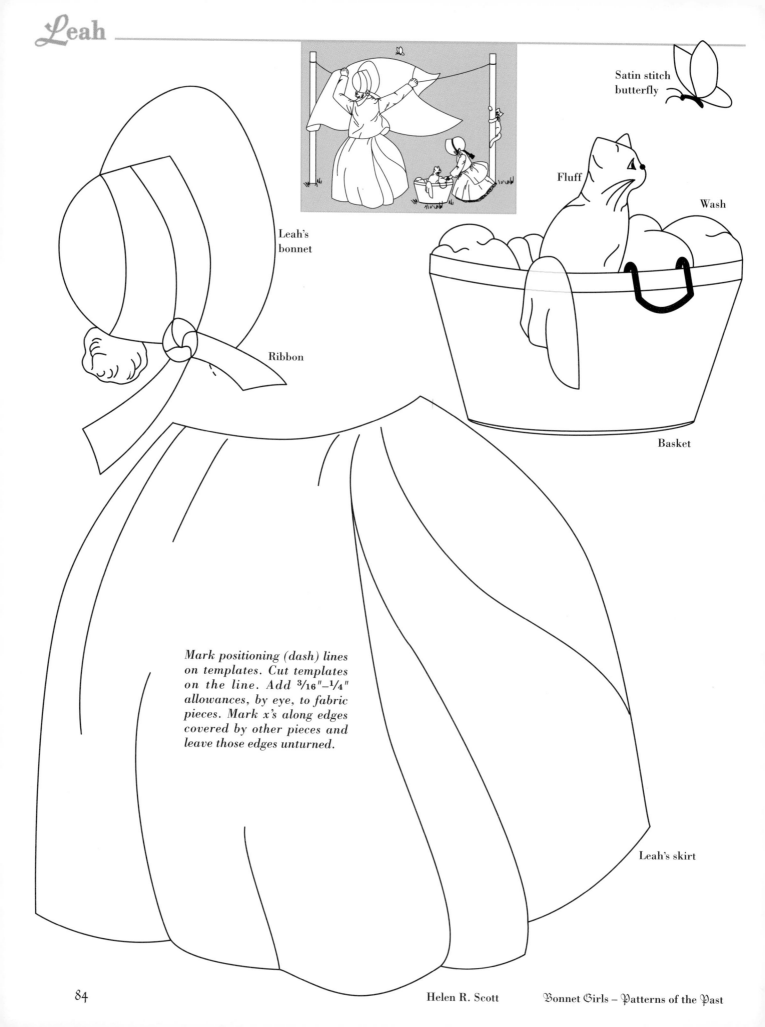

Satin stitch butterfly

Leah's bonnet

Fluff

Wash

Ribbon

Basket

Mark positioning (dash) lines on templates. Cut templates on the line. Add ³/₁₆"–¹/₄" allowances, by eye, to fabric pieces. Mark x's along edges covered by other pieces and leave those edges unturned.

Leah's skirt

Helen R. Scott   Bonnet Girls – Patterns of the Past

To assemble:
Baste turn-under allowance and press
Leah's bonnet, jacket, and four blanket
pieces. Baste bonnet and jacket together,
fit over four blanket pieces, pin together,
and baste to quilt block.

Nanny

Nanny is in a hurry to get her charge home before a shower becomes a storm. The block was quilted with diagonal lines and raindrops to indicate the coming storm.

I found a basket-weave fabric for the carriage body, but a solid or print would work as well. Keep in mind that it should be light enough to allow the fancy wrought iron frame to be visible. I don't like to use black floss on my quilt blocks. To me, it detracts from other embroidered areas. I prefer navy or dark blue and, in some cases, dark brown floss. Because Nanny is dressed in blue, a dark blue floss was chosen for the carriage frame. The wheels were outlined with dark blue (one strand) with a lighter blue-gray split stitch, two rows side by side, made with three strands of floss as a filler. Use metallic floss to outline stitch the spokes of the wheels and satin stitch the hub.

Fabric Requirements

Small patterns (as given): Use scraps for appliqué and embellishments. Block finishes 14" x 19". Cut background, backing, batting 15½" x 20½".

Enlarged patterns (155%): Use fabric measurements below. Block finishes 21¼" x 28½". Cut background, backing, batting 22½" x 30".

Figure	Fabric		
Face and hands	3" x 3"	Blanket	4" x 6"
		Pillow	2" x 3
Nanny			
Dress, sleeve, and bonnet	14" x 11"	***Embroidery***	
Apron, cuff, and collar	6" x 7"	Carriage frame, handle, and wheels	
Shoes	2" x 2"	Blanket fringe	
Hair	2" x 2"	Baby's face and hair	
Baby			
Body	2" x 3"	***Embellishments***	
Dress and cap	3" x 4"	16" of ¾" ribbon or lace for Nanny's bonnet	
		2" of ¼" lace for baby's bonnet	
Props		7" of ½" lace for carriage parasol	
Carriage	9" x 6"	2" x 3" piece of lace to cover pillow	

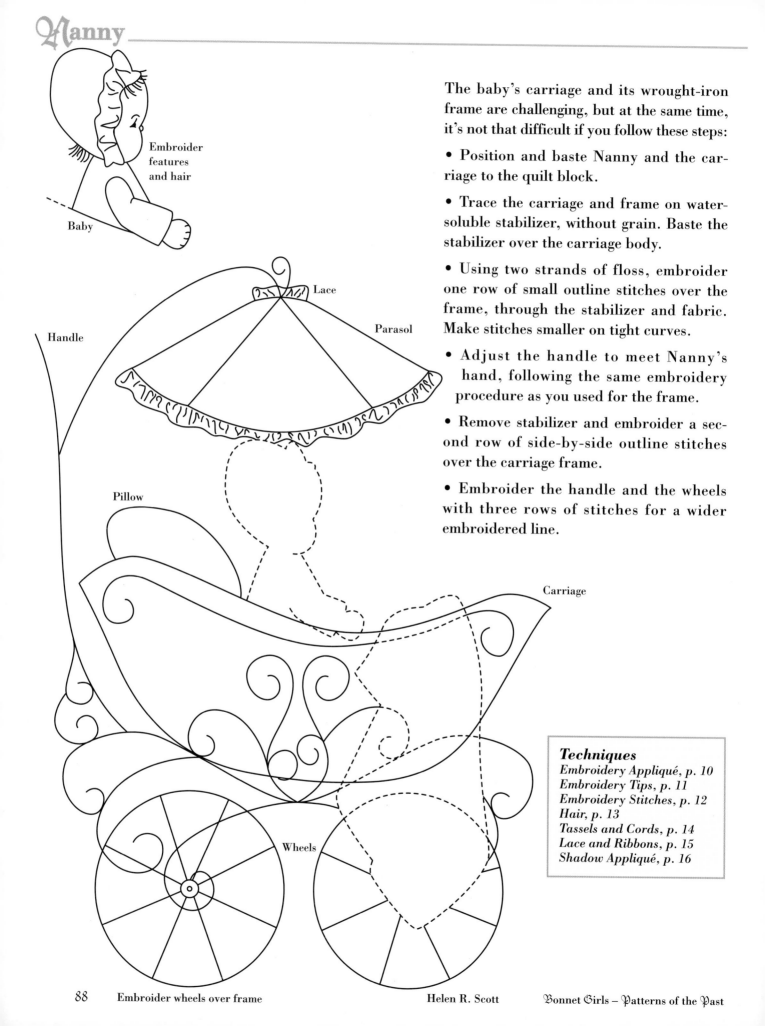

Embroider features and hair

Baby

Lace

Handle

Parasol

Pillow

Carriage

Wheels

The baby's carriage and its wrought-iron frame are challenging, but at the same time, it's not that difficult if you follow these steps:

• Position and baste Nanny and the carriage to the quilt block.

• Trace the carriage and frame on water-soluble stabilizer, without grain. Baste the stabilizer over the carriage body.

• Using two strands of floss, embroider one row of small outline stitches over the frame, through the stabilizer and fabric. Make stitches smaller on tight curves.

• Adjust the handle to meet Nanny's hand, following the same embroidery procedure as you used for the frame.

• Remove stabilizer and embroider a second row of side-by-side outline stitches over the carriage frame.

• Embroider the handle and the wheels with three rows of stitches for a wider embroidered line.

Techniques
Embroidery Appliqué, p. 10
Embroidery Tips, p. 11
Embroidery Stitches, p. 12
Hair, p. 13
Tassels and Cords, p. 14
Lace and Ribbons, p. 15
Shadow Appliqué, p. 16

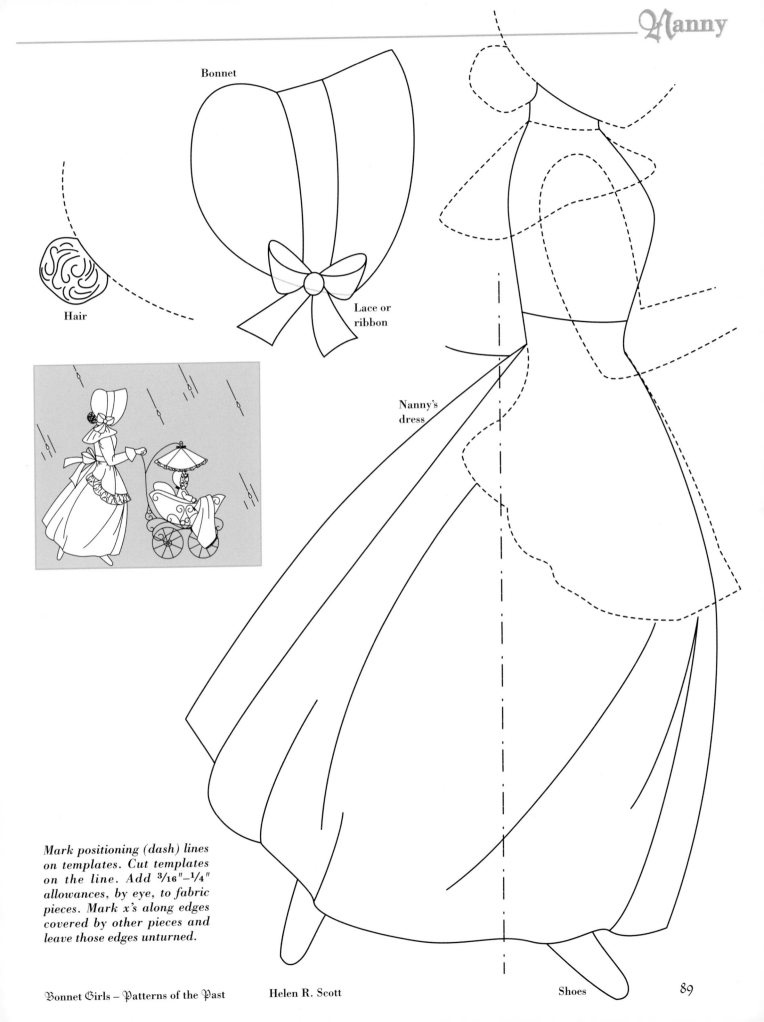

Bonnet

Hair

Lace or
ribbon

Nanny's
dress

*Mark positioning (dash) lines
on templates. Cut templates
on the line. Add ³⁄₁₆"–¹⁄₄"
allowances, by eye, to fabric
pieces. Mark x's along edges
covered by other pieces and
leave those edges unturned.*

Quilt slanted lines
and raindrops

Nanny's
collar

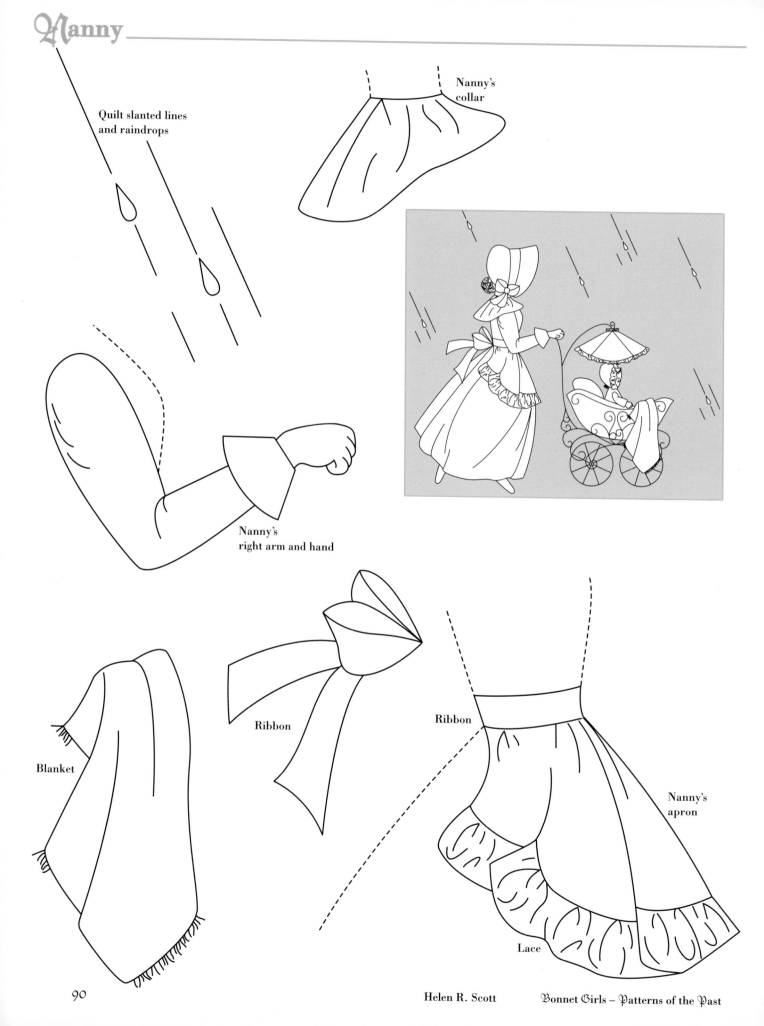

Nanny's
right arm and hand

Blanket

Ribbon

Ribbon

Nanny's
apron

Lace

Helen R. Scott   Bonnet Girls – Patterns of the Past

Yesterdays
Some days are meant to be held in special memory-places. To be taken out and savored. To be relived for the sweet taste that lingers. For bright echoes of laughter and the warmth of love freely expressed, freely given, and gratefully received.

Norma has cooked a Thanksgiving feast for her family, and young Josh is eager to sample the plump, steaming turkey.

The fabric for Norma's skirt was reversed. It was the right color, but Massie, the dog, was lost in the busy print. Many prints are just as pleasing on the wrong side as the right. Her apron is a piece of 7" lace tied with ¾" straight lace. A touch of blue in her blouse gave me the color scheme for the block, Josh's clothing, and the tray to hold the turkey.

Luke holds his feathered headband from which he has lost a feather to Massie. The feathers and band are satin stitched. Luke's hair was cut from a lion-print fabric. Massie is a skye terrier and is a dark, almost black, gray. He has long hair, which nearly covers his face. Artistic license can always be exercised to make him a color to fit your color scheme.

Your block need not be a Thanksgiving setting. Let Norma hold a candle, birthday cake, or quilt, or have her push a baby carriage. Blue and white striped fabric was used for the shadow appliqué to balance the block and complete the indoor setting. Your block could be pieced or appliquéd on printed fabrics.

Fabric Requirements

Small patterns (as given): Use scraps for appliqué and embellishments. Block finishes 9½" x 14". Cut background, backing, batting 11" x 15½".

Enlarged patterns (155%): Use fabric measurements below. Block finishes 14¼" x 21¼". Cut background, backing, batting 15½" x 22½".

Figure	Fabric
Face and hands	4" x 5"
Norma	
Skirt	11" x 12"
Trim and blouse	6" x 9"
Cap	4" x 4"
Hair	3" x 3"

Josh	
Jacket	4" x 6"
Pants	3" x 5"
Shoes	3" x 3"
Hair	3" x 3"

Props	
Massie	5" x 6"
Turkey	3" x 4"

Embroidery
Headband
Feathers
Josh's features
Massie's face

Embellishments
6" of 7" lace for apron
12" of ¾" lace for apron strings

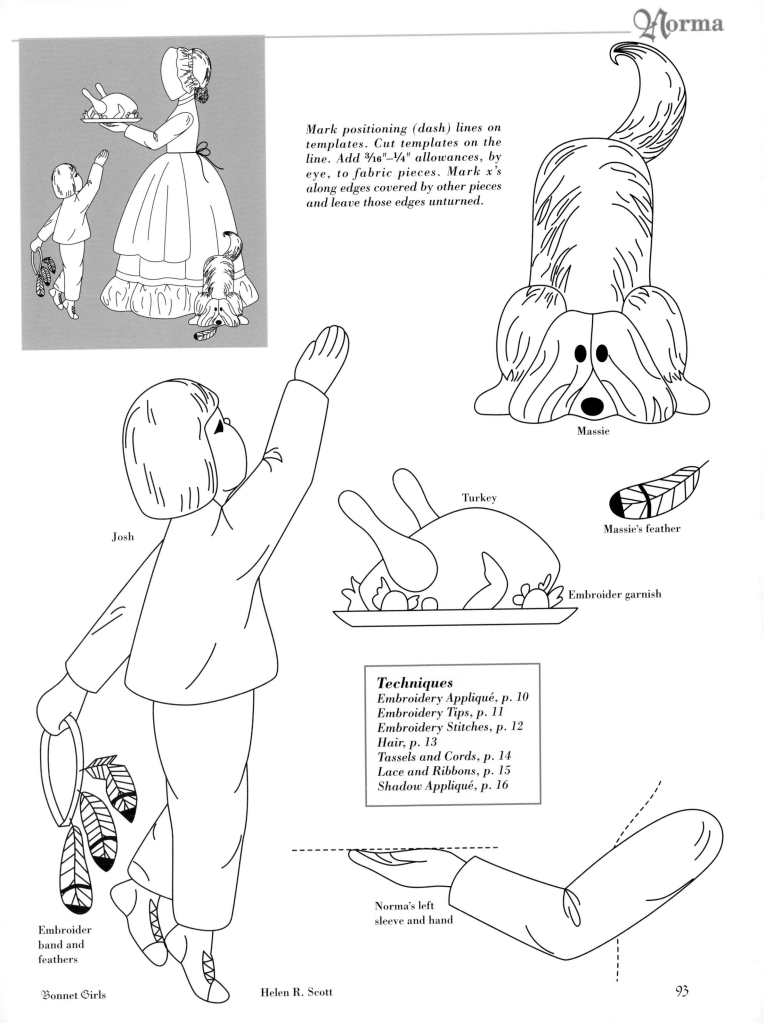

Mark positioning (dash) lines on templates. Cut templates on the line. Add ³⁄₁₆"–¼" allowances, by eye, to fabric pieces. Mark x's along edges covered by other pieces and leave those edges unturned.

Massie

Massie's feather

Turkey

Embroider garnish

Josh

Techniques
Embroidery Appliqué, p. 10
Embroidery Tips, p. 11
Embroidery Stitches, p. 12
Hair, p. 13
Tassels and Cords, p. 14
Lace and Ribbons, p. 15
Shadow Appliqué, p. 16

Norma's left sleeve and hand

Embroider band and feathers

Bonnet Girls   Helen R. Scott

93

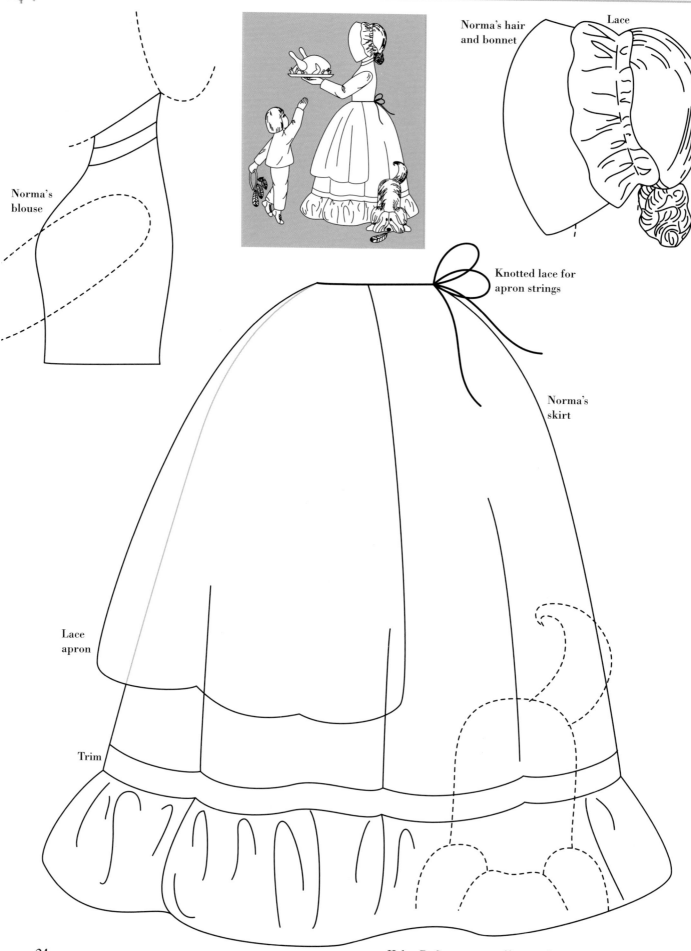

Norma's hair
and bonnet

Lace

Norma's
blouse

Knotted lace for
apron strings

Norma's
skirt

Lace
apron

Trim

Helen R. Scott   Bonnet Girls – Patterns of the Past

BOOOOO
Crickets sing the melody,
frogs are croaking base
bats are flying high and low
cover up your face!

Black cats howl atop the fence,
a witch soars on her broom
gnarled branches dance in
frenzied leaps beneath
the harvest moon.

Hurry home, Oh hurry home,
now goblins can be seen.
A ghost is lurking in the dark
tonight is Halloween!

Little Ghost wears a pale blue sheet to make him visible against the white background. Satin stitch his eyes and mouth. The pumpkins carried by Octavia and Little Ghost were cut from Halloween fabric and appliquéd to the block, but you could use plain fabric and embroider the details. I used shadow appliqué with dark turquoise and a yellow moon. Quilting lines follow the slanted lines of the clouds.

Fabric Requirements

Small patterns (as given): Use scraps for appliqué and embellishments. Block finishes 9½" x 14". Cut background, backing, batting 11" x 15½".

Enlarged patterns (155%): Use fabric measurements below. Block finishes 14¼" x 21¼". Cut background, backing, batting 15½" x 22½".

Figure	Fabric
Octavia	
Coat	11" x 10"
Skirt	9" x 10"
Hood	5" x 5"
Hand	1" x 1"
Little Ghost	
Sheet	7" x 11"
Props	
Pumpkins	4" x 7"
Cat	3" x 4"
Tree	4" x 11"
Moon	scrap
Shadow fabric	6" x 15"

Embroidery
Faces
Cat's face and tail
Pumpkin stems and details
Spider web and spider

Embellishments
French knots for coat buttons

Octavia's
hood and mask

Pumpkin

Octavia's
hand

Octavia's
cloak

Cat

Octavia's
skirt

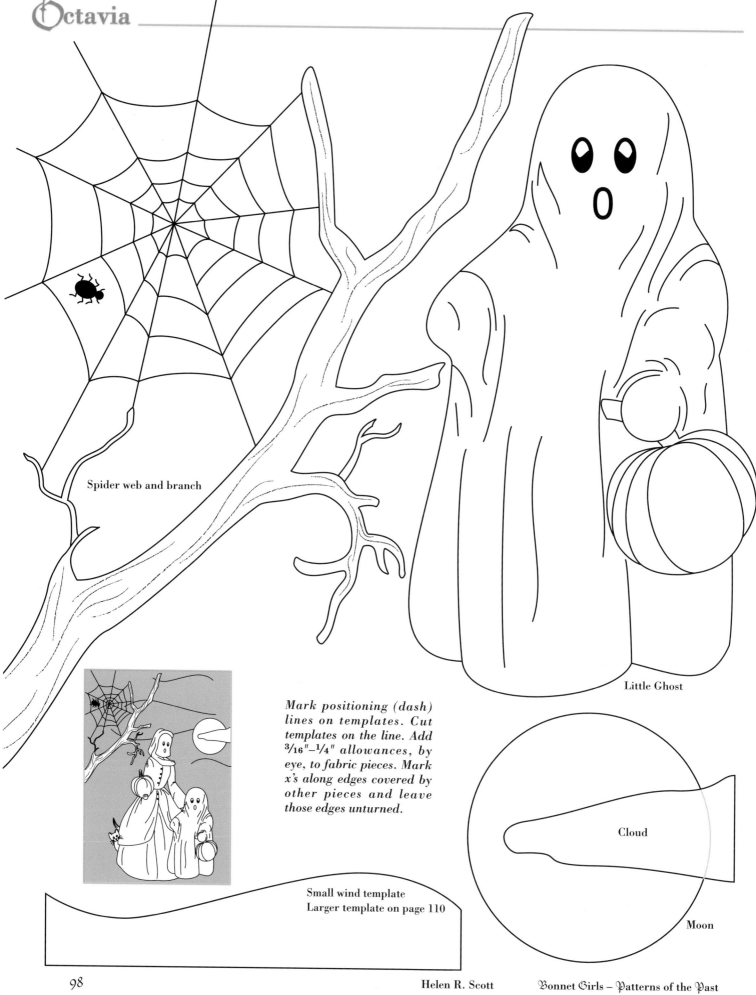

Spider web and branch

Little Ghost

Mark positioning (dash) lines on templates. Cut templates on the line. Add 3/16"–1/4" allowances, by eye, to fabric pieces. Mark x's along edges covered by other pieces and leave those edges unturned.

Cloud

Moon

Small wind template
Larger template on page 110

Daughter of My Daughter
This new little person, this woman child
Walking, running, dancing on new found legs.
Laughing at the wonder of her own ten toes.
Loving, hugging Mommy, Daddy, and Teddy bears,
with curls in her hair, Heaven's blue in her eyes, and
macaroni on her chin.
This Morgan Elizabeth, this new little person.

Morgan Elizabeth has had her bath and is ready to play with a doll offered by cousin Kristen. Trace Morgan on a piece of flesh-toned fabric large enough to fit in an embroidery hoop. Lightly trace her features: eye, chin, and ear. Use a thin mixture of light brown acrylic or fabric paint and, with a dry bristle brush, lightly brush on the hair color. Apply a warm yellow for a blonde, rust or orange for a red head. Dry and press.

You will find it much easier to tint cheeks and embroider features before cutting out the baby. If the flesh fabric is thin and the turned-under edges show, back the piece with flesh-colored fabric, cut on the line. Baste turned edges through all thicknesses. Press and baste the baby on the block. Use one strand of floss and varied sizes of small straight stitches to indicate hair.

I used a brown wood-grain fabric for Rachel's and Kristen's hair. The grain lines follow the direction of hair growth. Kristen has an embroidery floss "pony head," as she calls it.

This block was quilted in gently curved vertical lines. The wind template was turned end for end and reversed to mark the design. To carry color throughout the block, some vertical quilted lines were woven with one strand of embroidery floss.

Fabric Requirements

Small patterns (as given): Use scraps for appliqué and embellishments. Block finishes 9½" x 14". Cut background, backing, batting 11" x 15½".

Enlarged patterns (155%): Use fabric measurements below. Block finishes 14¼" x 21¼". Cut background, backing, batting 15½" x 22½".

Figure	Fabric
Rachel's and Kristen's hair	4" x 5"
Faces, hands, and Morgan's body	8" x 10"

Rachel
Skirt, sleeve, and bonnet	12" x 12"
Bodice	4" x 5"

Kristen
Dress	6" x 8"

Props
Doll	scraps

Embroidery
Faces
Doll's face, cap, hands, and legs

Embellishments
4" of 1¼" beaded lace for Rachel's bonnet
12" of ⅜" ribbon for Rachel's sash
12" of ⅜" ribbon for Kristen's sash
4" of 3½" lengths of floss for pony tail
3" of ¼" lace for Rachel's bodice
4" of ¼" knotted ribbon for Rachel's bonnet
30" baby rickrack trim for Rachel's dress, bonnet, and cuff

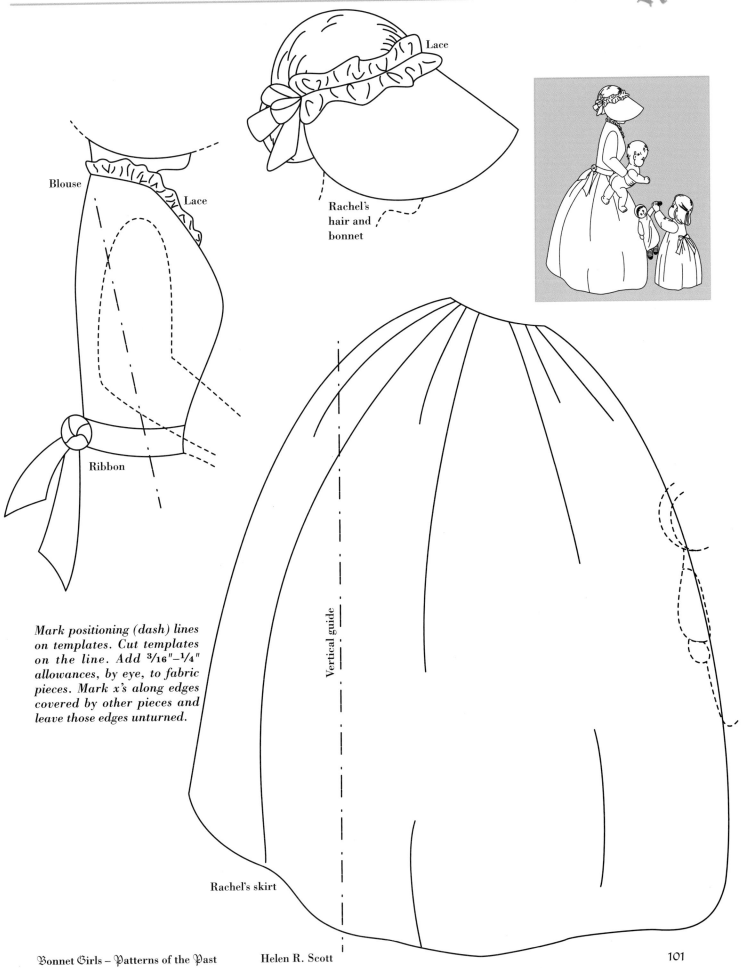

Blouse

Lace

Ribbon

Lace

Rachel's hair and bonnet

Lace

Mark positioning (dash) lines on templates. Cut templates on the line. Add ³⁄₁₆"–¹⁄₄" allowances, by eye, to fabric pieces. Mark x's along edges covered by other pieces and leave those edges unturned.

Vertical guide

Rachel's skirt

Kristen

Kristen's
doll

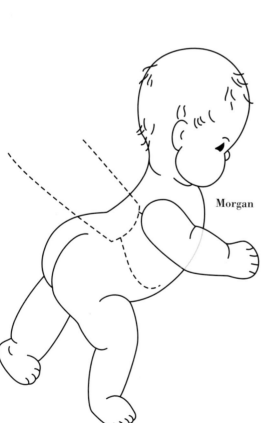

Morgan

Rachel's hand
without baby

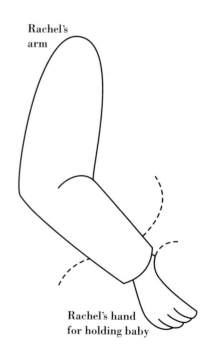

Rachel's
arm

Rachel's hand
for holding baby

Techniques
Embroidery Appliqué, p. 10
Embroidery Tips, p. 11
Embroidery Stitches, p. 12
Hair, p. 13
Tassels and Cords, p. 14
Lace and Ribbons, p. 15
Shadow Appliqué, p. 16

Early Risers

I felt the edge of spring today
A soft warm breeze, a roundelay.
The morning sun coaxed tulips red
to blossom in my flower bed.

Awaking oaks wear tender green.
New grass grows tall, and in between
stark winter's cold and summer's heat,
white melting snow and crocus meet.

Blue skies host clouds that quickly change
from feathered white to gray-dark rain,
and thunder storms rumble loud
to waken daffodils that crowd
in golden groups with violets blue,
for winter's gone, spring's born anew.

April Rose

The fabric for April Rose's dress was a gift from a friend. The lavender violets and spring greens brought to mind this poem I had written several years ago. Choose a spring fabric that will complement the block that precedes it in the quilt.

The dusty pink tulips and matching ribbon used in the sash, cuffs, and umbrella top brought out the touch of pink in the dress fabric. Soft tan was chosen for the sleeves, bonnet, and striped underskirt. Something brighter would have detracted from the floral print of the dress. Pink embroidery stitches along the bonnet lace and underskirt trim, the pink tulips, and the ribbon atop the umbrella carried pink throughout the block.

Quilted rain lines and drops complete the April theme. Mark the first rain lines from the upper-right corner to the lower-left corner of the block. Vary the lengths from 2" to 5". Use these lines as guides for marking other parallel lines and the raindrops. Some quilted lines and drops were woven with light blue-green floss to accent them.

Fabric Requirements

Small patterns (as given): Use scraps for appliqué and embellishments. Block finishes 9½" x 14". Cut background, backing, batting 11" x 15½".

Enlarged patterns (155%): Use fabric measurements below. Block finishes 14¼" x 21¼". Cut background, backing, batting 15½" x 22½".

Figure	Fabric
April Rose	
Dress	12" x 16"
Sleeves and bonnet	6" x 10"
Under skirt	5" x 3"
Props	
Umbrella top	4" x 7"
Umbrella underside	4" x 7"
Flowers	scraps

Embroidery
Tulip stems
Metallic floss for French knots at neck line
 and umbrella handle.

Embellishments
22" of ⅜" ribbon for sash, bow, and cuffs,
 umbrella top
6" of 1¼" gathered lace for bonnet and
 collar
6" of ½" gathered lace for hem

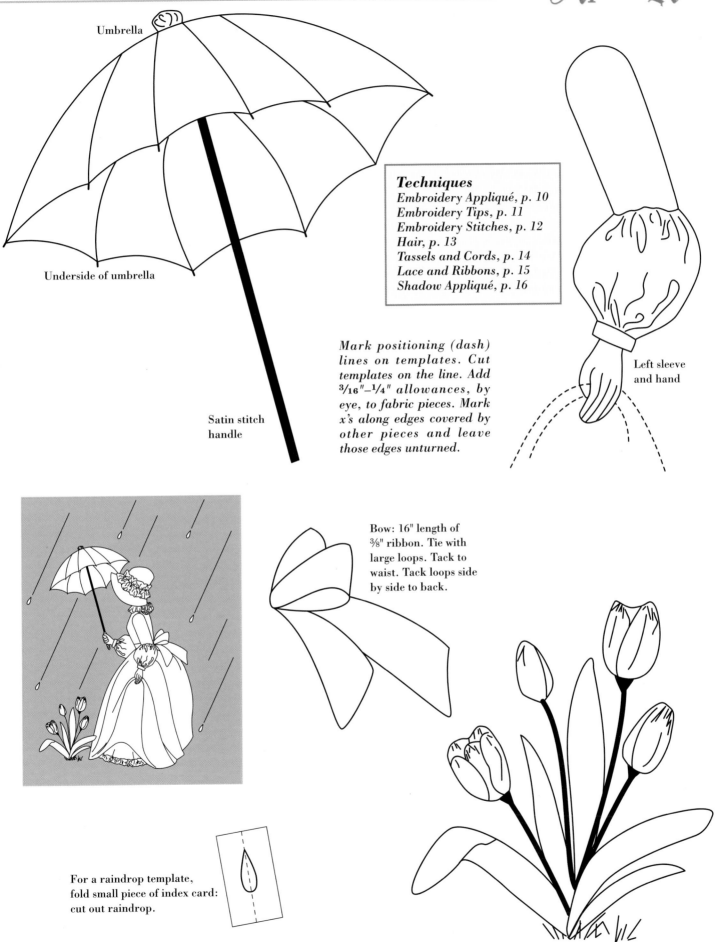

Umbrella

Underside of umbrella

Satin stitch handle

Techniques
Embroidery Appliqué, p. 10
Embroidery Tips, p. 11
Embroidery Stitches, p. 12
Hair, p. 13
Tassels and Cords, p. 14
Lace and Ribbons, p. 15
Shadow Appliqué, p. 16

Mark positioning (dash) lines on templates. Cut templates on the line. Add 3/16"–1/4" allowances, by eye, to fabric pieces. Mark x's along edges covered by other pieces and leave those edges unturned.

Left sleeve and hand

Bow: 16" length of 3/8" ribbon. Tie with large loops. Tack to waist. Tack loops side by side to back.

For a raindrop template, fold small piece of index card: cut out raindrop.

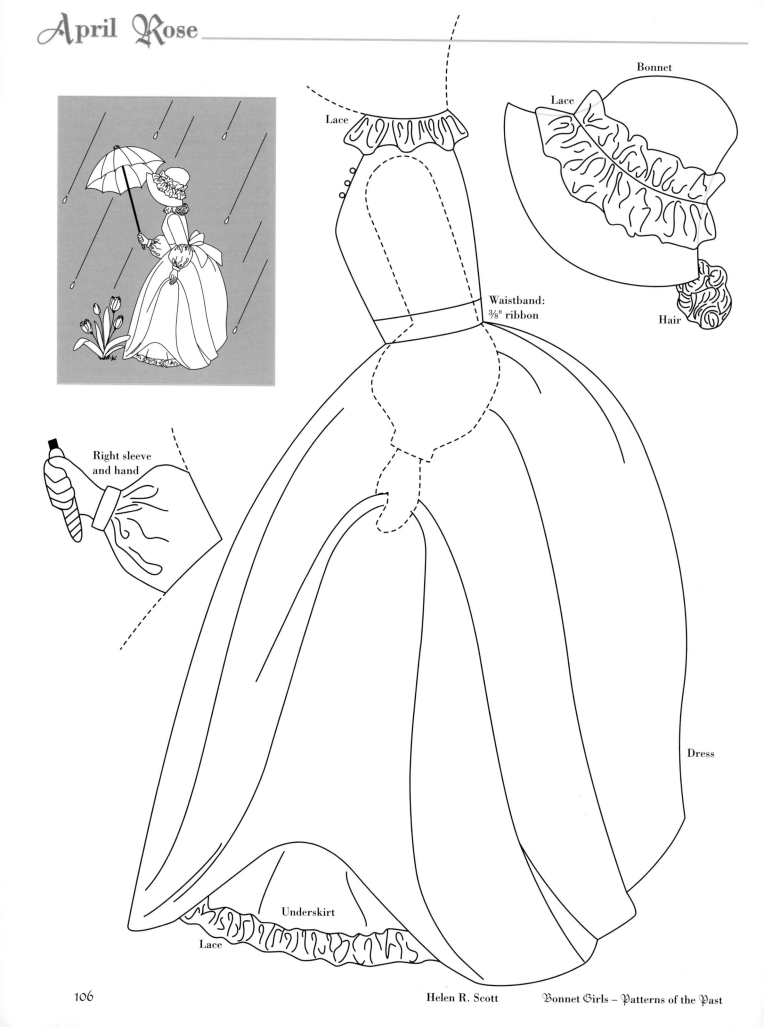

Bonnet

Lace

Lace

Hair

Lace

Waistband:
⅜" ribbon

Right sleeve
and hand

Dress

Underskirt

Lace

Helen R. Scott   Bonnet Girls – Patterns of the Past

View 1   *View 2*   *View 3*

Drew is always ready to greet or help a lady. As with the Bonnet Girls, he can be used to design a family tree, a seasonal block, or a theme quilt. With minor changes in position and the aid of props, he can accompany any Bonnet Girl. He can sit in on Miss Janet's arithmetic class, help Isabella trim the tree, present a gift or flowers to a special lady.

The body of the jacket is used for all three views. It is tilted for View 1, reversed for View 2, and used straight for View 3. Four hand patterns can tip a hat, hold a cane or candle, or wave to a Bonnet Girl or child. Sleeves and hands can be interchanged, raised or lowered, enabling you to create the pose or action needed for your theme. Props from the Bonnet Girl patterns, such as books, animals, candles, ornaments, and flowers will help you create new situations and groupings.

Fabric Requirements

Small patterns (as given): Use scraps for appliqué and embellishments. Block finishes 9½" x 14". Cut background, backing, batting 11" x 15½".

Enlarged patterns (155%): Use fabric measurements below. Block finishes 14¼" x 21¼". Cut background, backing, batting 15½" x 22½".

Trousers	4" x 7"
Shoes	3" x 5"
Face and hands	4" x 5"
Hair	4" x 4"
Props	
Hat	4" x 5"
Umbrella	2" x 6"
Scarf	7" x 4"

Figure

Figure	Fabric
Jacket	9" x 9"

Embroidery
Cane or umbrella handle and hatband

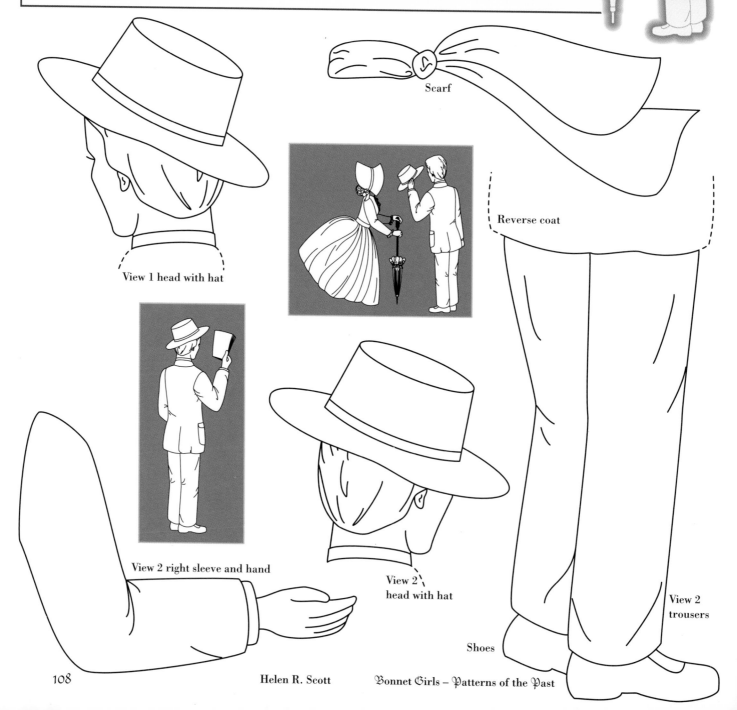

Scarf

View 1 head with hat

Reverse coat

View 2 right sleeve and hand

View 2 head with hat

View 2 trousers

Shoes

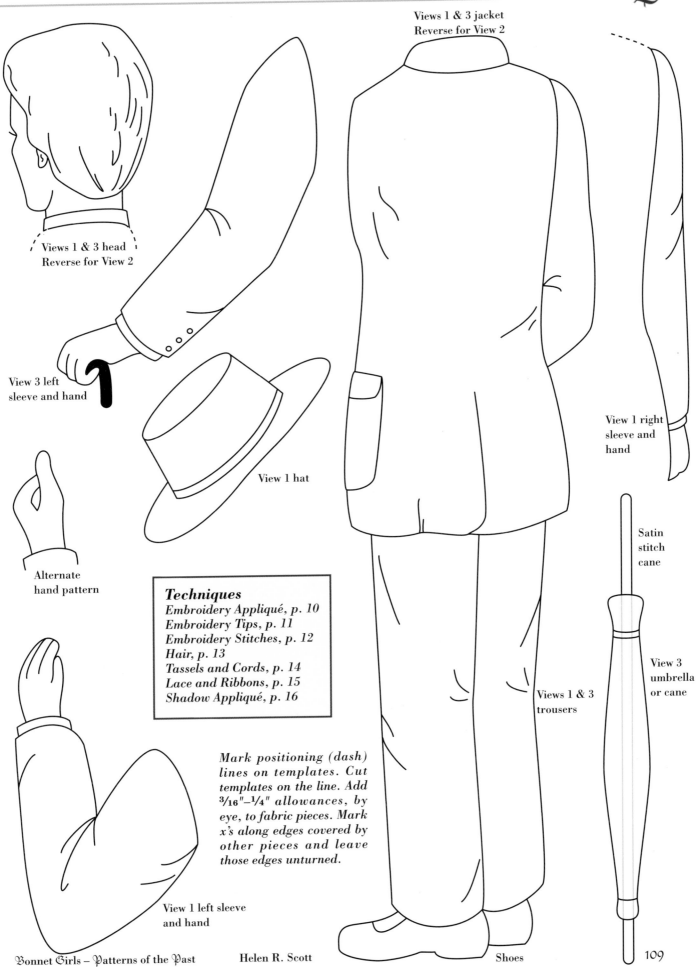

Views 1 & 3 jacket
Reverse for View 2

Views 1 & 3 head
Reverse for View 2

View 3 left
sleeve and hand

View 1 right
sleeve and hand

View 1 hat

Alternate
hand pattern

Satin
stitch
cane

View 3
umbrella
or cane

Views 1 & 3
trousers

Techniques
Embroidery Appliqué, p. 10
Embroidery Tips, p. 11
Embroidery Stitches, p. 12
Hair, p. 13
Tassels and Cords, p. 14
Lace and Ribbons, p. 15
Shadow Appliqué, p. 16

*Mark positioning (dash)
lines on templates. Cut
templates on the line. Add
3/16"–1/4" allowances, by
eye, to fabric pieces. Mark
x's along edges covered by
other pieces and leave
those edges unturned.*

View 1 left sleeve
and hand

Bonnet Girls – Patterns of the Past

Helen R. Scott

Shoes

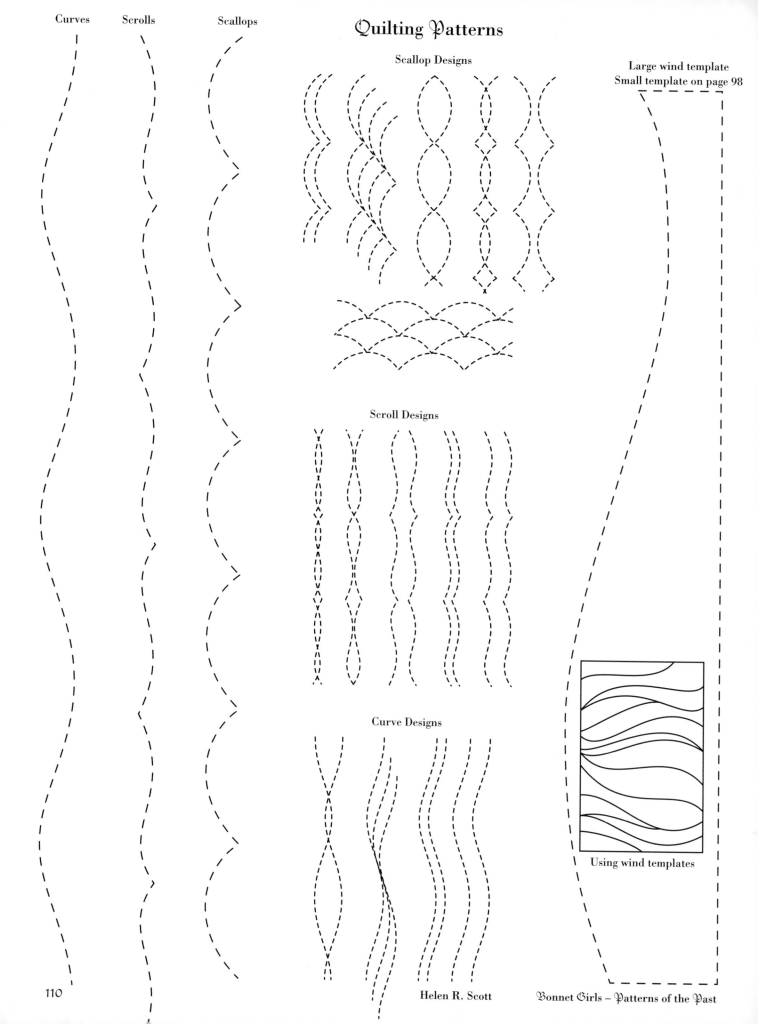

Curves   Scrolls   Scallops

Quilting Patterns

Scallop Designs

Large wind template
Small template on page 98

Scroll Designs

Curve Designs

Using wind templates

Helen R. Scott

Bonnet Girls – Patterns of the Past

About the Author

Some of my earliest memories are of playing under my grandmother's large quilting frames. There she worked on her quilts and those made by my mother and aunts.

When I started quilting in 1960, I chose appliqué. Having painted with oils, pastels, and watercolors for many years, I found that appliqué was like painting with cloth.

I started teaching embroidery appliqué and quilting classes in 1982. Using my original patterns, I held the classes at various places, including the Southern Ohio Museum; Shawnee State University in Portsmouth, Ohio; and Ohio University, Athens. I have made well over 50 quilts, using my own designs and a variety of subjects, as well as 14 theme quilts and wallhangings from the old-fashioned "Bonnet Girls: Gentlewomen" pattern series.

Other AQS Books

This is only a small selection of the books available from the American Quilter's Society. AQS books are known worldwide for timely topics, clear writing, beautiful color photos, and accurate illustrations and patterns. The following books are available from your local bookseller, quilt shop, or public library.

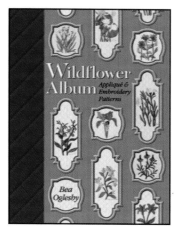

#5757 $19.95US

#5855 $21.95US

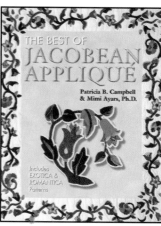

#5588 $24.95US

#5706 $18.95US

#5760 $18.95US

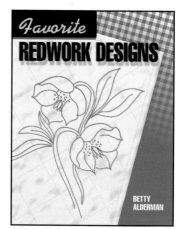

#5331 $16.95US

#5338 $21.95US

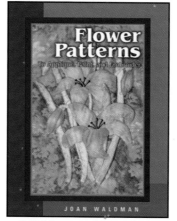

#5238 $19.95US

#5013 $14.95US

Look for these books nationally or call 1-800-626-5420